Bowhunting
MEGA BUCKS

Michael Hanback

©2004 Michael Hanback
Published by

kp books
An imprint of F+W Publications, Inc.

700 East State Street • Iola, WI 54990-0001
715-445-2214 • 888-457-2873

Our toll-free number to place an order or obtain
a free catalog is (800) 258-0929.

Library of Congress Catalog Number: 2004092783

ISBN: 0-87349-880-1

Designed by Jon Stein
Edited by Joel Marvin

Printed in the United States of America

Front cover photo by Lucas Strommen.

Contents

Acknowledgments

I will not list by name the pros that made *Bowhunting Mega Bucks* the gem that it is. You know who you are. Our readers will know how amazingly good you are at bowhunting whitetails once they finish reading this book. I believe your opinions and perspectives on mature bucks, along with your in-depth advice on how to find them and hunt them, make this the best work ever published on archery hunting for deer. Thanks, guys, for your time and help. Thanks for writing big chunks of these chapters and talking with me on the phone for hours, all of your work for free. Thanks for taking me hunting with you from time to time, and for footing most of the bill. Thanks for all the laughs on the road, in camp and in stands across our great country. Most of all, thanks for your friendship.

I'm of the opinion that a writer should never pen a book on any type of hunting until he first pays his dues and publishes hundreds of magazine articles on the subject. With that in mind, I owe special gratitude to: Todd Smith and Colin Moore of *Outdoor Life*; Gerry Bethge of *Whitetail Hunting Strategies*; John Zent, Frank Miniter and Scott Olmsted of the NRA's *American Hunter*; Bill Bynum of *Cabela's Outfitter Journal*; and Tom Fulgham, with whom I worked at *American Hunter* two decades ago. You guys are my favorite editors, and you have given me the chance to connect with millions of deer hunters across the country. You also helped to pay the bills as I ran around and chased big bucks in as many places as I could. Also, to my editor at KP Books, Joel Marvin, a hearty, "Job well done!"

I also need to thank Toxey Haas, Darrell Daigre, Ronnie "Cuz" Strickland, Mary Jane Orman and all the good people at Mossy Oak camouflage for believing in me and throwing their weight and support behind his book. One thing I have learned about the Mossy Oak folks is that they are not only hard-core bowhunters, but also some the leading conservationists and deer/land managers in the country. Working with them and some of their best hunting pros to bring you *Bowhunting Mega Bucks* was an honor and a pleasure.

About the Author

Ten years old and growing up in rural Virginia, Michael Hanback started firing wooden arrows at paper plates tucked under the twine of hay bales stacked in his granddaddy's backyard. As a teenager, he went from a recurve bow to a compound and killed his first deer. Now 30 years later, Hanback has chased elk, sheep, moose and most other species of big game across North America. But one of his passions remains the hunt for big whitetails. Hanback goes for mega bucks in five to 10 states and Canadian provinces each season.

He writes about those adventures for some of the country's top outdoor magazines. Hanback is a columnist and feature writer for *Outdoor Life, American Hunter, Whitetail Hunting Strategies* and *Cabela's Outfitter Journal*. He has penned six books, including *Modern Whitetail Hunting* (Krause Publications, 2003).

Hanback appears regularly on Mossy Oak's videos and television shows, including *Hunting the Country* and *Mossy Oak Classics* on the Outdoor Channel. He hosts the popular "Hunting Skills" segment on the *American Hunter* TV series. You can check out his new website at *www.michaelhanback.com.*

Introduction

In my not-so-humble opinion, I say you have just cracked open the best book ever published on archery hunting for whitetail deer. I say that not so much because I wrote it, although for 25 years I have chased the great animals on magazine and TV assignments across North America. But the true value of *Bowhunting Mega Bucks* lies in the extraordinary advice of the 13 hunting pros I collaborated with on the project. I have shared road trips, camps, laughs, scouting runs and long hours in tree stands and blinds with most of these guys. I'll tell you this. Each one knows big deer and how to kill them with a bow and arrow as well as anybody on earth. Want proof? The gurus have spent a combined 300-plus years tuning bows, reading sign, hanging tree stands, blood-trailing bucks and the like. As a group, they have arrowed hundreds of Pope and Young deer, from pretty 130-inchers to gnarly 10-pointers in the 160-inch range to monsters in the 190- to even 200-inch class.

I figured the best way to cover all the bases was to assign each pro a chapter on a particular aspect of the sport. I'd let them take the ball and run with it, and I'd interject a few points here and there. Well, I got what I bargained for and a whole lot more. Their opinions, perspectives and methods turned out to be candid, fresh, in-depth and *awesome*. For example, from the get-go in Chapter 1, tackle whiz Warren Strickland says, "I strongly endorse one of the new drop-away rests. It allows for more aggressive helical arrow fletching that promotes better broadhead flight." On the subject of lazy, fat bucks in warm October, Kentucky legend David Hale offers, "More so than a big temperature drop, I believe a falling barometer associated with a weather front is what makes old bucks get up and move. Watch your barometric pressure and hunt on afternoons when it starts going down." Later on, Mark Drury, who is 20 feet up a tree somewhere in the Midwest every day of bow season, points out, "We often see more big deer moving in December than we see in October and even during the November rut. I'm talking about $4\frac{1}{2}$- to $5\frac{1}{2}$-year-old giants with racks that score 140 to 160 inches and up."

All the techniques and procedures found in *Bowhunting Mega Bucks* will make you better regardless of where you hunt. No matter where he lives, an old buck is an old buck—crafty, unpredictable, secretive and to some degree nocturnal. But there is no doubt whitetails adapt and tweak their routines and movements according to regional differences in terrain, food sources, cover, and people and predator pressure. So working with pros Dan Perez (Midwest), Neil Dougherty (Northeast), Darrel Daigre (South) and Luke Strommen (West), I assembled chapters with specialized strategies for the various parts of whitetail country. I feel certain that pointed advice will help you kill more deer around home.

I wrapped the book up with an extended section on land management, which continues to be one of the hottest topics in the whitetail world. But I was determined not to give you the same old run of the mill advice on cutting a few trees and planting a few food plots. Again, I wanted fresh and innovative stuff, and I got it from the pros. For instance, camouflage guru and die-hard deer manager Jim Crumley suggests planting a good number of saw-tooth oak trees on your property. "Unlike other native white and red oaks, saw-tooths bear a reliable crop of big, meaty acorns each year," he notes. "The nuts fall in mid to late September and deer eat them through October, so you've got some great bowhunting opportunities." Also, Neil Dougherty's specialty is to design, build and plant green plots of an acre or less for ultra-close bow encounters with bucks. He tells you how to position the tiny, irregularly shaped plots across your land to take advantage of the predominant winds, the best cover and the major deer movements. Gems like that set *Bowhunting Mega Bucks* apart from all the other whitetail books on the market.

Sit back and give our book a good read. Refer to it in coming years as you plant your food plots, scout, tune your compound, shoot in the backyard, hang tree stands and on and on. Remember, you are getting more than 300 years of big-buck wisdom from some of the best bowhunters in the world. Let me go out on a limb and say right now: Once you've finished *Bowhunting Mega Bucks*, you can't help but to see and shoot more gnarly-racked whitetails.

Hunt hard and safely,
Michael Hanback

Chapter 1

Rigging For Whitetails

BACK IN THE GOOD OLD DAYS you could stroll into the local sporting goods store, pluck a hundred dollar bill down on the counter and walk out with a laminated-wood recurve, six field shafts, three broadhead-tipped arrows, a cool-looking quiver and a leather shooting glove or tab. You were good to go for whitetails. You might even pocket a little change.

"That was my first investment in 1972 when I purchased a Browning Nomad and a quiver of wooden arrows," recalls Warren Strickland of Owens Crossroads, Alabama. "That was one pretty bow, the envy of the neighborhood at the time."

Things were a lot simpler then. There were not nearly so many bows on the market, and the differences between the early spartan models were not that great. Selections of arrows, broadheads and accessories were minimal. Rigging up for deer hunting was no big deal.

Today, of course, the archery world has gone wild. Mega sporting goods chains, local bow shops, mail-order catalogs and Internet sites are jam-packed with an incredible array of bows, arrows, sights, rests, broadheads and other accessories. Jargon like "center shot" and "force draw curves" are standard fare in archery magazines and books. Talking heads on the Outdoor Channel and hunting videos toss around tech terms like "archer's paradox" and "harmonic-dampening systems." It is surely enough to intimidate the fledgling bowhunter, and at times enough to confuse the seasoned veteran. It is why, no matter your level of expertise, you need to follow these guidelines for setting up your whitetail rig.

Dr. Warren Strickland says your buck-hunting bow should have a nice mix of reliability, speed and forgiveness.

Bow Characteristics

An estimated 95 percent of deer hunters tote a compound with a let-off of 65 percent or greater. Although early wheel bows were plagued with frequent mechanical failures and excessive noise, today's high-tech cam models "are the tri-athlete of modern archery," according to the expert bowman Strickland. "When set up and tuned properly, they provide not only speed and durability but also arrow-splitting accuracy."

How a bow balances and feels in your hands goes a long way to how well you'll shoot it and how many deer you'll kill with it.

Too many people purchase a bow for all the wrong reasons. It is typical today for a guy or gal to buy a high-tech, super-short model based on speed alone, with the thinking "the faster the arrow the better." Others pick a bow with all the latest bells and whistles simply because it looks pretty and sexy. A buddy might like one particular bow so much that you figure you ought to shoot it too.

Well, when you're in the market for a new truck, you shouldn't look at just one slick Chevy or Toyota. You ought to shop around and check out several brands and models to see which one suits your needs the best. You certainly wouldn't buy a vehicle without a test drive! The same applies for a deer bow.

"I always recommend purchasing from a reputable archery pro shop," says Strickland. "That might require going out of your way and driving a long distance to a shop you like and trust, but I promise it will be time well invested."

For one thing, you can visit a shop and feel, draw and aim three, five or more of each year's cutting-edge models. How a bow balances and feels in your hands goes a long way to how well you'll shoot it and how many deer you'll kill with it. You can and should ask a pro-shop guy 100 questions about each bow's distinctive features. By all means, try to walk out back and shoot arrow after arrow through various display models.

As mentioned, these days, a common and often costly error is to consider only one of a bow's characteristics: speed. Several other factors are more important, namely durability, reliability, accuracy and forgiveness. "A nice balance of these four things is essential in creating a blue-chip hunting rig," notes Strickland. "Ignoring any of them can result in many hours of frustrated shooting and lots of wasted dollars."

When most people consider a hunting bow, durability and reliability are way down on their list of crucial features. But according to Strickland, they should be at the top. "Compounds generate a tremendous amount of kinetic energy, and as such, they must be engineered under strict quality con-

Short bows are the craze, but many hunters shoot better at targets and deer with a 36- to 39-inch-long compound with a brace height of 7.5 to 8 inches. To maximize a bow's speed and accuracy, try carbon arrows with mechanical broadheads.

"When you're cold and excited in a tree stand and your form is less than perfect, it helps to have a forgiving bow that will compensate a little when you shoot at a big buck," says Strickland.

trol and with the most durable materials available. The limbs are particularly vulnerable. Before purchasing any bow, talk to several owners of that brand and ask about any mechanical failures. Consistent problems among different people usually reflect a fault in design. Regardless of how accurate or forgiving a bow is, if it spends more time in a bow press than out of it, it isn't a good investment."

The forgiveness of a compound refers to its ability to tolerate or compensate for a shot that you do not perfectly execute. "Even the most experienced shooters are guilty of an occasional lapse in form and technique," notes Strickland. He goes on to point out that when your technique is less than perfect, say when you're 20 feet up an oak on a cold day with a pounding heart and a monster 8-pointer standing broadside 20 yards below, it sure helps to have a bow that will help compensate a little when you loose an arrow.

Certain compounds by nature of their compact design are notorious for being intolerant and unforgiving. Here's one big thing to remember in this era of ultra-short, super-fast compounds: "The shorter the bow and the lower the brace height, the more intolerant the setup is to a break in your shooting form," says Strickland. "That's why target shooters prefer longer bows with higher brace heights, which make for a less sensitive and more forgiving setup."

Hunting-wise, it begs the question: Is one of today's lightning-fast bows with an axle-to-axle length of only 30 to 32 inches right for you? If you practice year-round and have great shooting form most of the time, the answer might be yes. But if, like many hunters, you shoot a few weeks or a month before whitetail season, you're probably better off with a longer, slightly heavier and more forgiving bow.

Visit an archery shop and shoot several super-short display models. If one of them feels especially good and if you can drive arrows like tacks with it on the 3-D range out back, go for it. There's no doubt that a short, lightweight compound is easy to wield and maneuver on the ground and especially 20 feet up a tree. However, you might shoot best with a 34- to 36- to 39-inch bow.

The brand or cost of a bow doesn't matter. "To shoot well, you just need a forgiving bow that fits you well and has a reasonable draw weight," says Strickland, shown here with another monster 10-pointer.

If so, buck the super-short craze and hunt with a longer bow.

That is precisely what Strickland has done. "I have never been able to realize the advantages of the pygmy power-houses," he says. "I still prefer a hunting bow with an axle-to-axle length of 36 to 39 inches and a brace height of 7½ to 8 inches. That gives me excellent forgiveness, if modest arrow speed, for my whitetail setup."

Once you've exhausted your search and settled on a bow, have your pro-shop guy make sure it fits you *precisely*. "That's the first key to smooth and accurate shooting at targets or at bucks," notes the Alabama pro. "For some reason, most people purchase bows with draw lengths that are much too long. That results in inconsistent anchoring and poor back tension when you draw and hold the string, and it often leads to very poor accuracy." Remember, by simply shortening your draw length half an inch to an inch, you're apt to shoot a whole lot better, be it at foam deer or live bucks.

These days many hunters jog and lift weights, which is great. But some guys get a little buff, start thinking they're Schwarzenegger and run out and buy bows with titanic draw weights. That can be a huge mistake. "A draw weight that is too heavy results in a breakdown of your shooting form when you struggle to draw and hold, especially in a tree stand, and that contributes to inconsistent or poor accuracy," notes Strickland, who in addition to being an expert shooter and hunter is also a practicing physician. "Shooting too much poundage markedly increases your chances of a serious muscle injury."

Shooting Straight

A highly forgiving and accurate rig is just as critical in the woods as on a 3-D range. Sometimes a giant buck just materializes beneath your tree stand; you're rushed to make a quick shot count. To do it, you must often lean around the tree or contort into an unorthodox position. You might be faced with a hostile environment, say rain, sleet, wind or bitter cold. Your knees will wobble and your heart will pound in your chest at the sight of the magnificent creature. The last thing you need is a finicky setup. "These are the very real reasons I will

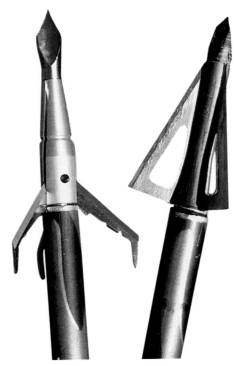

Mechanical or fixed-blade broadhead? Hunt with the one you shoot best and in which you have the most confidence.

accept nothing less than ultimate forgiveness and field-point-like accuracy with my hunting bow, arrows and broadheads," says Strickland.

Accuracy is measured in two dimensions: horizontal and vertical. Because bucks often show up at unknown or tough-to-pin-down yardages – no matter how freely you use your laser range finder – the vertical component is of particular interest. Trajectory and arrow velocity are the main determinants of vertical accuracy. The flatter the arrow trajectory and/or the higher the velocity, the more room for error when shooting at a buck, whether he is at 18, 23 or 26 yards.

The horizontal plane is more sensitive and temperamental. We're talking about arrows that might group to the right or left of center. There are certain characteristics of a compound that can help enhance side-to-side accuracy. One of the most important is a center-shot riser. Such a riser is cut past center to allow string, arrow and rest to be aligned at absolute center without an arrow's vanes contacting the bow face. This markedly improves arrow flight and horizontal grouping. This innovation is now standard equipment on all modern compounds.

The design of a bow's handle is also an important link in the accuracy chain. Big, bulky grips transfer considerable torque from the riser to the archer's wrist, sometimes resulting in arrow groups to the left or right of center. Strickland finds that the addition of a torque-free riser and a narrow grip can significantly decrease torque, thus improving horizontal accuracy. "Another smart add-on that combats left-right groups is a sight bubble or leveler," he adds. "A bubble helps you detect minute degrees of bow canting that can be detrimental to your horizontal accuracy."

The arrow rest is the most critical piece of equipment on a hunting bow. The ideal rest is easy to adjust, durable and provides 100 percent vane or feather clearance when you let fly an arrow. "You should definitely shoot and test several different rests before making your final selection," says the Alabama pro. "I prefer the new generation of drop-away rests. The addition of a properly set drop-away rest can make any deer hunting rig more forgiving and accurate."

The vast majority of problems you experience when tuning a compound can be traced to arrow/rest contact.

A fall-away model virtually eliminates this problem, especially when shooting carbon arrows. "Also, a drop-away rest allows for the use of more aggressive helical-type fletching that promotes better broadhead flight," notes Strickland. "I strongly endorse this type rest on any hunting bow. Blow it on rest selection and you are in for hours of frustrating shooting."

The 65-percent let-off wheel has greatly improved the accuracy of hunting compounds. Higher let-off means a lower holding weight, and that allows for more precise aiming and, in the end, flawless shot execution. This advantage is gained with a minimal loss of kinetic energy as compared to lower let-offs. The 65-percent let-off wheel has gained wide acceptance with deer hunters and is now considered standard equipment on most compounds.

Due not only to its accuracy and forgiveness but also its ease of tuning, the Solo-cam has gained extreme popularity with today's archers. Once plagued with unacceptable low velocities, this cam design is now capable of similar velocities as generated by dual cams. Just recently, the hybrid "cam and a half" has taken the archery world by storm. Strickland is impressed. "This cam design offers the best of both the Solo and dual-cam worlds," he says. "The cam-and-a-half design just about eliminates timing problems that can affect accuracy. It also provides an extremely forgiving, fast and accurate setup. Anybody looking for a new whitetail rig should seriously consider the hybrid cam and a half and a new-generation drop-away rest."

Broadhead Flight

You know the drill. All summer you stand in your backyard and zing arrow after arrow into foam blocks and 3-D deer. Your confidence soars as you pluck shafts into an orange-size circle at 20 and 30 yards. You pump your fist and bark, "I'm gonna nail a big deer this year!"

One afternoon a few weeks before the opener, you switch from 100-grain field points to three-blade broadheads of the same weight to put the finishing touches on your buck rig. Your first arrow sails four inches left! The next is way low! You keep firing and your arrows keep hitting the fake deer all over the place. You get flustered and start stomping around and cussing. It's one of the most exasperating and confidence-deflating aspects of our sport. Unfortunately, it's also one of the most common.

"The biggest reason for inconsistent broadhead flight is an improperly spined arrow," notes Strickland. "Usually you need an increase of one or two arrow spines above that previously used for field points for sound and accurate broadhead control."

An under-fletched arrow can also result in reckless flight. Although 2- or 3-inch fletching can produce excellent flight with field points, this is rarely the case with broadheads. "Most exposed-blade broadheads require 4- to 5-inch vanes or feathers on arrows," notes the Alabama pro. "And a helical configuration, while not as important for field points, is absolutely necessary with broadheads. The helical pattern allows for indispensable arrow rotation, and that's essential for dependable and consistent broadhead stability and accuracy."

A hunting head or nock misaligned on an individual shaft can also produce wobbly, accuracy-busting flight. Pull every arrow out of your quiver and spin it on the point of the broadhead. Turn the shaft over and spin it on the nock. If the arrow doesn't spin smoothly and true, you've got an alignment problem on one end. Fix that shaft or don't hunt with it.

As you can see, many factors can contribute to poor accuracy with exposed-blade broadheads. Because of that, Strickland says, "I'm convinced that even when these factors are corrected, these heads are rarely able to deliver field-point accuracy out of today's compound bows. Achieving acceptable hunting accuracy at speeds greater than 260 feet per second is difficult with an exposed-blade broadhead, especially one with more than a one-inch cutting diameter."

That is why Strickland has switched to mechanical heads for all his deer and big-game hunting across the country. "Going to an open-on-impact broadhead has delivered unparalleled forgiveness and accuracy to my hunting setup. The large cutting diameter of many expandable heads provides superior stopping power for even the toughest big-game animals. I've also found that open-on-impact heads produce superior arrow penetration, though some people might not agree. If you're after the ultimate in accuracy and forgiveness, you really ought to try them."

Though you might get away with a marginally tuned bow with field points, that's not likely with any style of broadhead. Shoot your hunting heads through paper to test and possibly correct faulty nock height or center shot. Powder-test the fletching of your arrows to make sure they clear the rest with room to spare.

Without a doubt, improper tuning is the most common reason for a lack of forgiveness and/or poor accuracy with a deer-hunting bow. Problems might be due to unsynchronized wheels, improper center shot, under- or over-spined arrows, a misaligned nocking point or a similar little gremlin in your setup.

"With all that in mind, it's easy to see why the expertise of a first-rate pro shop really shines," notes Strickland. "Properly setting up and tuning one of today's high-tech compounds require the skill of an ardent, experienced archer. He's usually found at the nearest pro shop."

Tackle Tips:

> To set the nock point on a new string, nock a shaft, lay it on the arrow rest and level it perfectly. Mark the string at the top of the arrow and clip the nock point right there.

> Clip your release to the string, close your eyes, draw your bow and anchor. Open your eyes. You should be able to see the fiber-optic sight pins clearly through the peephole without moving your face, anchor point or bow. If not, let down and adjust the peep slightly up or down.

> When changing a bow's draw weight, never apply extreme torque to the big bolts or you might damage the limbs. Turn each bolt lightly and exactly the same.

> Wax your bowstring every two weeks during peak practice time, or anytime you notice a little fraying. Replace a string when wear is evident or every 2 years under normal shooting conditions.

> Lightly lube a bow's axles where they pass through the cams every 1500 to 2000 shots. When hunting in dusty or rainy weather, lube wheels and cams daily. Use a silicone- or Teflon-based lubricant.

> Carry a 9-key hex wrench in your pack for tightening quiver, overdraw, sight and arrow-rest screws. Check screws periodically during bow season.

> If you still shoot three-blade heads, carry a plastic broadhead wrench for tightening and tuning them to your arrows.

> If you're not using a laser rangefinder, you're hunting in the dark ages. Climb into a tree stand or ground blind and check various landmarks within 20 and 30 yards. Try easing up your optic and lasering any does or small bucks that walk by. In some situations, if the cover and approach of a good buck are just right, you can range him before you draw, ensuring that you'll pick the right sight pin and tripling your odds of making a double-lung shot.

> After climbing into a stand, check for debris in and around your bow's cables, split limbs and cams. Weeds, brush or twigs from the hike in or the rope up can get jammed into your bow and cause trouble.

> Carry an extra armguard in your pack. If you lose your original on the hike in, you can switch to your backup to flatten your coat sleeve and keep it from grabbing your bowstring on a shot. More importantly, never leave home without an extra release aid. If you drop your number one release from a tree stand, you can dig out your spare and salvage a hunt in seconds without having to climb down.

> Screw fixed-blade or mechanical broadheads into the six hunting arrows you'll carry in your quiver. Shoot every arrow into a broadhead target. You'll undoubtedly find that two or three of those arrows fly smoother and more accurately than the rest. With a Sharpie, mark those shafts one, two and three. Those should be the first three arrows you hunt with.

> When sighting in and adjusting pins, "follow the group." For example, if your arrows hit right of center, move sight pins right. If arrows hit low, move sight pins down.

> Try arrows fletched with white or yellow vanes. I've found that when you shoot a deer, your eyes will instinctively follow brightly blurred fletching. Watch precisely where vanes or feathers disappear into a buck, and you'll have a good idea of the trueness of the shot.

Chapter 2

Scouting for Mega Bucks

Jim Crumley loves to scout thickets between feed fields and white-oak ridges. That's where he shoots a lot of big deer, like this white-antlered giant.

ONE DAY A COUPLE OF YEARS AGO out in the big-buck woods of southern Illinois, Jim Crumley shivered as he watched a giant rise from his bed, push through a thicket and spill out into the open timber more than a long bowshot away. The barrel-chested 9-pointer with a rack the color of bleached bone tilted back his head, lip-curled and looked out into a nearby food plot. The rut was fixing to bust loose any day now, and the stud was keeping both visual and olfactory tabs on the local hotties. Not seeing or smelling much of interest, the white-tined brute skulked back to his bedding hole.

A short time later the deer got up, went through his sniff-and-peek routine again and lay back down. Hmm, maybe the third time would be a charm. The big boy

15

In late summer, glass for bachelor groups of bucks in hayfields, clear-cuts and the like. At least one shooter will live nearby when bow season opens. Lucas Strommen photo.

popped out of the thicket once more, glanced out into the field and seemed to surmise that no does were ready to hook up in this part of the woods. As the buck walked off to check another section of his core area, he bore straight for Crumley's perch.

"I could hardly believe it at first, but then a big deer coming on that trail was my hope and intention all along," he says. "My biggest concern was grabbing my bow and settling my nerves for a good shot."

He did fine, smoothly drawing at the right time and smoking the 150-incher in the boiler room.

Crumley set the stage for one of his best kills by scouting and finding what he calls a "parallel trail." Such a path rims the perimeter of many food plots and crop fields across the country, generally running some 20 to 50 yards back in the timber. Some trails are sections or feeders of main doe runs, while other paths are off on their own and used only by a buck or two.

"Many of the trails are so faint you'd hardly even know they're there," notes Crumley. "The only way you might know is because you spotted a good buck in the same small area a couple of times, like I did with that big Illinois deer."

You can shoot a buck on a parallel trail anytime of the season and especially during the rut. Whether on his home turf in west-central Virginia or out in Illinois, where he hunts some years, Crumley hones in on the trails in early to mid November. That's when rubbing, scraping, testosterone-crazed bucks use parallel trails most heavily. They typically walk the paths on the downwind sides of plots or crops, smelling and looking out into the open feeding areas for does. If a gal smells right, Mr. Big might then bust out into the open to nudge or chase her. You need to try to stick him before that happens.

One way to do it is to hang a tree stand 20 to 30 yards deeper in the woods and downwind of a parallel trail. For example, if the wind blows out of the northwest one evening, a buck should check for does on the southeast side of a plot. You need to be in a stand 20 yards or so off that parallel trail, a little further back in the woods to the southeast.

A perfect strategy is to set a stand on a long, relatively open hardwood ridge, a place where horny bucks love to travel and scent-check for does in the first place. On a hogback, you can not only cover a parallel trail out front, but you can also see any deer that move out in the plot or up and down the ridge. During the wild phase, you might spot deer from the perch morning, noon or afternoon.

If two or three days in a row you spot a buck walking or cutting a trail 70 to 100 yards away, you might need to tweak your setup. "But it takes a lot of seeing a big deer in one particular spot before I'll move my bow stand," says Crumley. "I believe that most of the time you're probably better off sitting tight. A buck might come down that trail anytime."

Now on to more advanced scouting pointers, and how to use them for more 20-yard shots at mega bucks.

Pre-Season Plans

Crumley watches deer and keeps his eyes open for sign as he works his Virginia property in the spring and summer, bush-hogging, planting, fertilizing or whatever. In late August, he gets down to business. He walks logging roads, trails and field edges, and he glasses up into the tops of oaks to see which trees bear a heavy crop of green nuts. Just as importantly, he notes which trees have so-so mast and which are barren for the year. "Red, black, pin and chestnut oaks are all great and deer eat them, but I really focus on the white oaks. I'll pull stands off white oaks that won't bear and move them near trees that will drop lots of acorns in early bow season. Focus on white oak acorns wherever you bowhunt. Deer will walk past other food sources to get at them."

Above: Any scrape worth a second look will have a mangled lick branch dangling above it.
Left: Scout for white-oak acorns that are just beginning to fall and hang a tree stand nearby.

Knocking around his 296-acre tract during the summer, Crumley has a pretty good idea of how many bucks, and how many shooters, roam the place. On soft, sultry September evenings, he glasses to confirm all that, as well as spot other deer he hasn't seen before.

He has a pretty cool system. "I've got several tree stands where I can watch a strip-planted 20-acre field that is the hub of deer activity on my place," he notes. "But I do most of my scouting from a video house I built. I can sit, watch and tape deer that come down off the nearby ridges and show up in the strips of clover and Biologic." He goes home, studies the tapes of mature bucks and where they're coming out of the woods and starts putting together a plan for next month.

At this point, the pro has a good handle on the bed-to-feed pattern of his local herd. And having scouted the most productive white oak trees within a reasonable distance of his strip-planted field, he has a lot of options for October. He can hang stands downwind of the oaks or hunt his best traditional sets on the edge of the field. Either way, he is guaranteed to see whitetails. But he's not done scouting for feed yet.

"You need to check for all natural foods away from your food plots or strips," says Crumley. "We already talked about the acorns, but scout for persimmons, paw-paw, apples or whatever soft mast you have in your area."

Early on, you need to determine which fruit trees will produce, and you ought to hang one or two stands nearby. Some deer – and maybe the one shooter you've been watching all summer – might stage and feed on apples or persimmons for a few days or a week when bow season opens. "If you quit seeing a big buck in a plot or around acorns, he might be back in the woods hitting soft mast," points out the Virginia pro. "Sneak back into one of your secondary stands and give it a shot."

I hike over and check every good-size cedar I spot off in the distance. I often find it freshly blazed, sign that at least one shooter lurks in the area.

The only time you can shout "Old buck!" with reasonable certainty is upon finding a wide, deep track 3 to 4 inches long.

Rubs & Scrapes

Once Crumley has pinned down an area's food sources and bedding areas – "Most all the deer on my place bed high on rolling, 2000-foot mountains and ridges and move down to feed, so they're fairly easy to pattern," he says – the bulk of his scouting is done. But he bowhunts every day in October, and he pays attention to all the new sign that starts popping up in the woods.

"I like finding a big, fresh rub and fantasizing about the buck that made it," says the whitetail guru. "It's satisfying to think a deer 3½ years or older is working a corner of the property I'm managing. A big rub gives me the confidence I need to keep hunting in an area, even if I'm not seeing a lot of deer there."

Crumley believes the size of rubs is relative to the area you're hunting. "Out in Illinois where the giants roam, I've found rubbed trees the size of telephone poles. Back home in Virginia, a 4-inch rub gets my attention."

Look at it this way. If you're fortunate enough to

hunt a state and an area where a fair number of 140- to 170-class whitetails prowl, scout for huge rubs that mark some segment of a monster's core area. On the other hand, if you bowhunt a property where a 120- to 130-class buck is a shooter, hone in on rubs as round as a coffee cup.

In some areas, bucks like to blaze certain species of trees. Knowing that can make your scouting more efficient. "On my Virginia property, 90 percent of the rubs I find are on pine, cedar and poplar trees," notes Crumley. "Here's something interesting. Bucks love to thrash small pines, but I rarely find a big rubbed pine. Ninety percent of the time a large rub is on a good-size cedar."

In my experience, that holds at least partially true from Alabama to Iowa to New York. If I'm out scouting a new piece of ground anywhere in the country and spot a cedar patch or a lone cedar off in the distance, I stop the truck and hike over to investigate. More times than not I'll find a fresh aromatic rub or an old blaze from a season past. Either way, it tells me a good buck was once in the area, and he's probably still there. I'm of the notion that in most regions these days, a big deer spends most of his time in a roughly 400- to 600-acre core area.

As for scraping, Crumley finds it can vary from year

Clay in soil can hold a track's sharpness for a day to a week, making it tough to determine its freshness.

to year and from area to area, depending on the sex ratio and the age structure of bucks in a herd. When he bought his property more than a decade ago, you couldn't find many scrapes. The previous landowner had shot only bucks for years, and there were way too many does on the place.

"Now, after years of management, there's a lot more scraping because there's a lot more competition among an older age-class of bucks. I find scrapes all over the place, especially on the edges of my food strips and beneath some saw-tooth oak trees I planted."

Crumley monitors the pawing as it starts and intensifies in late October and early November. It gives him an idea of when peak breeding is due to explode. But he is not a scrape hunter per se. He rarely, if ever, sets up over even the largest, dankest patches of dirt. "I pay more attention to the big rubs I find. Usually those rubs and scrapes are clustered in a hot area that you need to bowhunt."

Tracks & Trails

The Virginian does not believe you can conclusively determine the sex or size of a whitetail by its track. But,

"A fresh, trampled trail interests me any time of the season," notes Crumley. After finding one, he checks an aerial photograph for nearby food sources and bedding areas where does and bucks are headed or coming from. If the terrain and cover allow, the pro likes to glass a well-worn trail from a safe, scent-free distance in an effort to determine when and how deer are using it. "If I watch a trail two or three evenings and mornings in a row and don't see many animals, I figure most of the deer activity on it is at night, so I move on," he adds. "But sometimes the only way to know for sure is to sneak in, hang a climbing stand on a trail and hunt it a couple of days "

You might strike out, or you might surprise and stick a monster.

Trail Cameras

Trail-monitoring cameras have been around for decades, but they are enjoying a new boom with today's tech-savvy archery hunters. "Deer cams" are great for getting an idea of how many mature bucks live in your hunting area. They're even better for pinning down when, where and how those animals feed, travel and bed.

As a general rule, purchase one cam for every 100 acres you hunt. If you and your buddies can pool your funds and swing three

To get good buck photos, strap your cams tight to trails or within 20 feet of scrapes during the rut.

again, he realizes that things are relative according to where people hunt. In an Eastern or Southern region where middleweight, 120- to 130-class bucks are the norm, a deep, 3-inch track might indicate a buck or mature doe. But in Kansas, Iowa or Saskatchewan where 240- to 300-pound bruisers roam, an old shooter is likely to leave an exceptionally long, deep and splayed print. Check the direction of a fresh, gargantuan track and try to determine where a big deer is going. Take a chance and hang a stand for a quick-strike ambush. It's a simple tactic, but people run arrows through some monsters that way every season.

or four cameras, that's great. You can move them around, cover lots of terrain and photograph more bucks.

Start using your trail cams in late summer. You might snap a bachelor group of four or five P&Y bucks coming to a food plot in August or early September. Come October, they won't be far, so bowhunt nearby. A few of those deer should roam your area all season.

Leave your cameras running throughout the rut to see what transient bucks move into your area to steal some does. Move in and hunt a vagabond for the week right after you snap his photo, before he breeds a few gals and goes back home.

Montana outfitter Eliot Strommen ponders his next move. Note how the snaky Milk River and the dark points of timber where the bucks bed jump out at him at on the aerials.

Be scent free as you sneak in to hang cameras and check film and batteries (roughly once a week and during the middle of the day when most deer are inactive). Wear rubber or Scent-Lok boots, spray down with an odor-killer and approach a photography site from downwind.

The best pictures of bucks are generally snapped from 10 to 20 feet away. To get the tight shots, strap your cams 2 to 3 feet high on trees and in spots where the terrain or structure will funnel deer along a major trail. Close to a gap gate, a pond dam, a creek crossing, a woven-wire fence or a long brush pile are just a few good spots to set a cam.

Most mature bucks are photographed at night. The automatic flash on most cams works best when an animal is 9 to 15 feet away, so, again, set up close to a trail or rub line.

Set a cam facing across a trail rather than straight down it. The camera's motion sensor will work better, and you'll get good broadside shots of bucks.

Some of the best shots you'll ever get will be at fresh scrapes at night. It couldn't hurt to hang a scent wick or dripper to lure in bucks.

Make sure no leaves or brush are between a camera's lens and a trail or scrape where you plan to "shoot" a buck. Swaying vegetation can falsely trigger a camera's heat/motion sensor. Also, carry a compass and set a camera facing to the north or south. It's best not to point one due east or west, where the rising or setting sun can trigger false shots, or wash out photos of deer. Avoid pointing a cam toward the sky. The open space and light will backlight and overexpose deer.

Be sure to record where and when you hang your cams and where and when you get shots of bucks. Cross

Scouting Tips:

➤ Every day you're in the woods either scouting or hunting, pack a journal and jot down everything you see, hear and find – a big 10-pointer in a plot, two bucks fighting in a thicket, a pine rub the size of a power pole, 30 scrapes on a ridge and so on. When you cross-reference your data against an aerial photo of your archery zone, you'll be surprised how deer patterns start to jump out. The more data you collect over a season and especially over several years of scouting and hunting the same property, the narrower and truer the buck patterns become.

➤ The more you glass an area the better off you'll be. Purchase the best 8X or 10X binocular you can afford. We're talking class glass like Leica, Swarovski, Zeiss, etc. You'll also need a 15X-45X spotting scope.

➤ Start observing deer in crop fields, hay pastures and open woodland areas in August and September. Glass every deer you see from a stand from October through December. Analyze where those animals are coming and going until yet more patterns emerge.

➤ Most times of the year, mature bucks love to bed high on hillsides and ridges with their backs to the wind, where they smell the rising thermals and scan the woods below for other deer as well as predators. But during the rut, don't overlook a monster that might lie up in or near an open woods or field where he can watch for does coming and going. Glass for a big rack moving in a fencerow, fallen treetop, brushy ditch, tall patch of weeds – you get the picture.

➤ A 2-acre brier tangle, a thick clear-cut, a strip of second-growth timber – again, you get the picture – will hold a few deer or a bunch of bucks at some point in bow season. Keep scouting thick edges for rubs, scrapes, trails and big tracks. The day they pop up, hang a tree stand close for a quick strike.

➤ Chances are a mature deer blazed a big rub, especially the first one you find in September or early October. But a few times, I've watched spindly-racked 6- and 8-pointers all pumped up during the peak rut shred good-sized trees, so don't be fooled. Still, most of the time the "big rub equals big buck" theory is reliable.

Glass a feeding area several days in a row, pattern the comings and goings of a big buck and move in for a quick-strike ambush when the wind is right.

reference the photos with aerial photographs and other data you've collected – maybe a big shed, sightings of a huge buck in a plot in September or big rubs you found on an oak ridge in October. Put it all together to get the big picture of where, when and how Mr. Big travels. Now you're ready to hang your bow stands and get him.

Big-Buck Shocker

The day after Crumley arrowed that 150-inch Illinois buck that you read about in the beginning of this chapter, he was back in the woods with a doe tag burning a hole in his pocket. Climbing out of the truck and grabbing his gear, he recalls the outfitter telling him, "This is one of our best doe stands. Shoot straight."

Crumley climbed into the tree and rigged up the small video camera he carries on every bowhunt. He didn't have to wait long for action. A muscle-bound buck with a gigantic rack stepped out of the woods and swaggered along the edge of a green plot! The monster

- Look for small rubs that line out from a sign-post and connect a buck's feeding and bedding area. Rub lines are tough to find when the foliage is thick in early bow season. But still-gleaming rub lines jump out at you on a post-season scout in January or February. If food sources and covers remain pretty much the same, that same buck or another bruiser should roam the same general route next fall.

- Trampled doe trails that wend from thickets to fields and run through draws, drainages and other funnels are definitely worth following and investigating. Keep in mind that major doe paths change as food sources ripen and dry up, and as hunting pressure builds in an area. Bucks prowl along and across doe paths throughout the fall and especially during the rut. Look for trail crossings, which are often marked with fresh rubs and/or scrapes. Those are excellent spots for bow stands.

- Climb a ridge or hill that rises 20 to 50 feet above a grass or CRP field. Or hook a climbing stand to a straight tree on an edge and work your way up. From up high, glass the field and study how gouged-out deer trails parallel, cross and re-cross. You'll be surprised how visible the paths are. With vital knowledge of how deer cross the field, you can slip over to an edge and hang a stand for a high-odds ambush.

- The most reliable way to tell if a mature buck ripped a scrape is to look around it. A couple of big, fresh rubs near a scrape are the best indicator of a shooter.

- It's pretty easy to tell the freshness of a scrape in dirt – dry and brown is old, while black and moist is hot. But along a river or anywhere in the Deep South, a day-old scrape in sandy soil might look a week old. More times than not a sandy scrape is fresher than it looks. Any serious scrape has a mangled "lick branch" overhead.

- "On many woodland tracts, the first rubs and scrapes of October pop up in and around logging roads, so scout those first," notes Crumley.

- Biologists say that a deer defecates about 24 times a day. If you find a lot of scat beneath an oak tree or in a nearby honeysuckle thicket, some deer are feeding or bedding there. The old saw that the bigger the pellets the bigger the doe or buck that dropped them is generally true. Check the color and texture of pellets when trying to decide where to hang a bow stand. Whitetails that eat apples, persimmons or other soft mast drop dark, moist clumps. Deer that feed on corn or acorns leave drier and lighter-colored pellets.

strolled within 18 steps of the doe stand. Crumley calmed his nerves, pointed his camera and got some great, close-up footage of the buck before he vanished.

The beast looked to be at least 6½ years old and to weigh about 300 pounds. His gargantuan 10-point rack had drops and stickers all over the place, and a 14-inch brow tine corkscrewed upward! Several experts who have studied Midwestern monsters for years, including Mark and Terry Drury, have reviewed the amazing footage and scored the rack from 205 to 215 inches. It is one of the largest whitetails ever videoed in the wild and possibly the biggest buck ever captured on film. The deer is still out there, having never been spotted since.

There are a couple of lessons to be learned here. First, consider carrying a small camcorder on all your hunts. You can have a ton of fun videoing does, squirrels, birds, coyotes – and shooter bucks that skulk by out of bow range. The more bucks you study on film, the better you'll get at field-judging body sizes and racks.

Secondly, and more to the point here, remember that regardless of how thoroughly you scout a property, you never know for sure when and where a giant buck will show up in daylight hours, especially during the rut. A beast might stroll past one of your best "doe" stands or walk smack under one of your "worst" buck posts. All you can do is put in a lot of time in the woods and hope for your own mega buck shocker. If and when it happens, hopefully you'll still have a buck tag left.

Chapter 3

The Ultimate Bow Stand

IN THIS SPORT, YOUR CORE TASK is to go out to a well-scouted spot and hang a tree stand for a cozy, broadside or quartering-away shot at a whitetail. The job is not nearly so easy as I just made it sound. In fact, it is your ultimate challenge during all phases of the archery season. If you do everything right but miss your mark by just 10 or 20 yards, you'll sit 18 feet or so up a tree and watch a buck glide by a whisker out of arrow range. That animal might be of Pope-and-Young caliber. Heck, he might even be a Boone-and-Crockett monster! It might be your one and only chance in life to score big. Talk about maddening! To keep your blood pressure in check and get more good shots at deer, you need to tighten up your setups.

In & Out

Any tree in which you even think about putting a stand should have easy and quiet access. "You can scout till the cows come home and find great trees in great spots blazed with fresh tracks, rubs and scrapes," says Terry Drury of Bloomsdale, Missouri. "But if the access to those trees is poor, you can't or shouldn't hunt them."

A straight, solid tree might be located too far from a field edge or logging road where a short, quiet hike to it isn't an option. If you clump too far through the woods, especially when the leaves are down and dry as Corn Flakes, you'll sound like an elephant and spook some deer. Also, a great-looking oak or hickory might grow on the wrong side of a thicket or a major trail that runs to it. If you try to bull your way to a stand and jump bedded or walking deer along the way, you've obviously messed up.

It's important to have a good exit strategy as well. After a hunt, especially in the evening, you should be able to climb out of a stand and sneak back to your truck without spooking too many deer. If you can't get out of a crop field or mast flat without clearing it of animals, it's not worth hunting that place because that ruckus will quickly cause an old buck to change his pattern. Pull that stand and re-hang it in a nearby spot with better getaway access.

Your goal should always be to slip quickly and quietly to and from a stand without disturbing a single deer. To do it, "Look for stand locations that are not too far off old roads, trails, power-line rights-of-way, etc.," notes

To get the drop on a gnarly buck, Terry Drury says first things first: "Choose a stand site with quiet and easy access."

It pays to hang your first stand well off a food plot or bedding area. After glassing and patterning a big deer for a couple of days, move in with another stand for the kill.

Run your steps far up a tree and step safely down into your stand. Strap in with a full-body safety harness.

the pro. "Plus, the water helps to rinse traces of scent off your boots."

As a rule for evening hunting, choose a tree with easy access from the food-source side. For example, sneak down the edge of an alfalfa field or clover plot early in the afternoon, turn a few yards into the woods and climb into a stand. You shouldn't bump a single animal. You certainly never want to angle cross country toward an afternoon stand along a brushy ridge or draw that runs from a bedding area back in the woods – you'll spook deer moving from the timber to the feed and ruin your hunt.

For morning hunting, try to find a tree near a bedding area that you can get to before dawn. "Sneak in from downwind as quietly as possible in the dark, climb the tree and get settled," says Drury, who goes by feel and the light of the moon (the guy never uses a flashlight). "Some deer in or near the cover might hear you, but they'll usually settle down before first light. By getting there extra early, you'll beat some bucks back to their beds. If a big deer comes skulking along at sunrise or later, you'll be 20 feet up a tree waiting for him."

You need to plan your in-and-out routes carefully, but a lot of it is trial and error. You might have to hang a stand and hunt it several times before you can determine whether or not your access works. After a few sits, analyze things. Did you sweat too much on the hike in? Did the walk take too long? Is the wind right or iffy? Did you bump any deer? You might go into a spot three or four times and figure out your plan is great. Or you might deduce that it just doesn't work. You might need to tweak your final approach to a stand, come in from an entirely different direction or choose another tree altogether. It's a continual learning curve.

Drury. "Or sneak to a tree along the edge of a pasture. Use aerial photos and topographical maps to determine the easiest and most convenient routes to stands."

Drury goes on to say that anytime you can creep up or down a creek or river, do it. Where he hunts and videotapes in Illinois and Iowa, many of the creeks have steep banks that can hide a hunter perfectly. "You can wade a creek toward a stand like you're strolling down Main Street without deer seeing or smelling you," says

Play the Wind

Every day that you scout or hunt a farm or woodlot, monitor the various wind directions at morning, midday and afternoon. Mark those wind currents on a map and in a journal. Over time, you'll determine the prevailing winds that accompany various weather patterns at different times of the year. That is vitally important info because the majority of the trees you pick for stands will be based on the most common winds.

A lock-on stand with a comfortable seat and a large base for your feet is the ticket for bowhunting.

This is one of the best bowhunting setups you'll ever see. Note how limbs hide the hunter by breaking his outline. Good cover behind your stand is most important.

Think! Deer couldn't walk through this barrier when entering or leaving the field; they'd have to circle around it. Your stand would need to be in a tree 30 yards off one end of the bale line where the wind is right.

"Where we hunt, south, southwest, west, northwest and north winds are most prevalent," says Drury. "So most of the trees we pick for stands are with those winds in mind. A straight east or northeast wind is rare, but we have a few trees selected for those winds just in case. You always want options, so hang enough stands that you can hunt on different winds."

You know to focus on spots where deer will likely come in upwind of your stand. That is important, but it is not enough. When picking a tree, you need to determine where to put your scent so you'll alert as few deer as possible in the area. If a mature buck circles in downwind of your stand and catches your stench, he might just melt away into the brush. But an ornery old doe might stand out there and stamp and blow for 15 minutes, bringing your blood to a boil and, worse, alerting every deer within a half-mile that something is bad wrong. Either way, your hunt is probably ruined.

"My brother Mark and I like to float our wind over a dead area that's probably not going to see a lot of deer traffic that day," says Drury. "Typically, we'll put our wind out into a pasture field, or maybe out over a creek or river that deer won't or can't cross."

Determining the best wind for a stand definitely involves some trial and error. You might look at an aerial, point your finger and bark, "Okay boys, a northwest wind will work best right there." But until you go in and sit the stand several times, you don't really know if a northwest is best or even adequate. You need to study the topography of an area because ridges, bluffs, draws and other terrain and foliage features can and do affect wind direction, sometimes dramatically. You also need to glass a lot and observe the overall deer movement throughout an area as it relates to various common winds. Most of the time, mature bucks work into the wind, or at least into a crosswind.

The Ultimate Bow Stand

A climbing stand offers great mobility. In the rut, I like to move in with one and hunt a ridge blazed with smoking rubs and scrapes.

More often than not, your instincts will be good, and your theory about the best wind or winds to hunt a tree will be on the money. Once you've hunted a tree a few times and feel confident you've pegged the best winds, stay with that strategy when planning daily hunts from season to season. Unless the terrain or cover changes (i.e., a landowner cuts or thins 20 acres of timber), those winds will hold true over time.

Now once in a while you'll be wrong. The breezes in a spot simply won't blow according to how you guessed they would. Again, it might be because of the topography or the thick or thin cover. And again, you've got to go in, hang a stand and sit in it for a few days to find out. You might have to tweak your setup and find another tree close by. Or you might have to vacate the spot altogether if the wind is just too unpredictable to get a 30-yard shot at a buck.

Drury bowhunts quite a bit on the ground, especially late in the season. A blind of cut cedars breaks a cold wind and offers great cover.

Most hunters concentrate on wind direction but neglect wind speed. Mistake! "Wind speed is just as important as wind direction," says Drury. He goes on to point out that he and Mark have stands on the tops of fields and ridges that are perfect for high-pressure mornings with low winds. They also have trees in draws and hollows that are just right for strong north or west winds that kick up after a front blows through. They go to those stands to get out of the wind and down into calm holes where the deer usually are.

These days, any hunter who doesn't log onto *www.weather.com* daily throughout bow season is screwing up. Type in the zip code of the town nearest your hunting property, and then click on "Hourly Forecast." Up will pop the 10-day weather forecast. Look closer and you'll find the very best info – an hourly forecast that gives you the wind direction and speed for the next 48 hours. It's a great tool for planning which stand to hunt because you know which direction the wind will blow one morning or afternoon. You'll know if the breeze is going to switch and, if so, when. You'll know if and when the wind is due to kick up or calm down. "We've found the weather.com data to be very accurate, and we use it daily," notes Drury.

Hang 'Em High

How high should you hunt? That depends first and foremost on the amount of cover in and around a tree says Drury. "We like some cover to the front and sides of a stand, but background cover is the most important. You always want to set up where limbs, leaves, forks, vines, etc. behind your stand help to break your silhouette."

Tree Stand Tips:

➤ Look for trees for stands at midday, when most does and bucks are bedded. A quiet, rainy day is perfect. Scout with the wind in your face or quartering over your shoulder to keep from spooking deer.

➤ At a new stand site, be quiet. Don't throw or bang steel or aluminum stands and steps around. If you're hanging with a buddy, don't talk or laugh too loudly. Set up and sneak out of an area without alerting deer that might be bedded or walking nearby.

➤ "Everybody looks for big, straight trees, but a hardwood that leans slightly back and toward your downwind side can be great," says Drury. "When you hang your stand on the 'up' or front side of the tree, it will be comfortable and positioned perfectly for shooting. The wind will be in your face or quartering on."

➤ It's always best to hang a stand perfectly level. When a tree is not truly straight, set the foot platform so that it tips slightly up. When you sit, this raises your knees slightly and makes you comfortable. When you stand to draw and shoot, you'll be firmer and safer than if the platform were to tip slightly down.

Given their druthers, the Drury boys like to hook a fixed-position stand 17 to 20 feet up a tree. "That's where Mark and I feel most comfortable," says Terry, who goes on to say that is the ideal height at which to shoot at a buck. "When a deer is broadside at 15 to 25 yards out and 17 to 20 feet below, you've got a great shooting angle. You can see plenty of the lungs."

Don't just stick a stand on a tree, but angle it to maximize your opportunities. "We always face our stands dead into the wind, or, at the very least, quartering into the wind," notes Drury. "That way, you'll see the most deer out front or off to the sides, and be ready to set up a shot at a buck. It just doesn't make sense to hang a stand anywhere on the downwind side of a tree. Why float your wind out over the same piece of woods where you're watching for a buck?"

Ground Attack

Often there is no large, straight tree within bow range of a field edge, thicket or narrow funnel where you've spotted a monster several times. Or you might find what looks to be a good tree for a stand, only to find that the wind, cover, visibility or shooting lanes are poor there. Well, don't sweat it. Go for a ground attack. More and more hunters are doing it these days, and they're killing some mighty fine bucks. "Actually, a lot of times you're better off on the ground than trying to squeak by in a marginal tree setup," adds Drury.

Most people worry about their scent when bowhunting at ground zero. Well, stop your fretting. On the ground, your scent doesn't travel as far, swirl as much or disperse and pool as widely as it does from a tree stand, so fewer whitetails might actually smell you. Of course, you still need to setup downwind of where you expect a buck to show up.

As you scout in the summer or walk to or from a favorite tree in the fall, always be on the lookout for a secluded spot where you might surprise a mega buck. "If we nail down the movements of a big deer through long-range observation, or simply spot a buck nudging a doe in an out-of-the-way place one day, we don't think twice about sneaking in and hunting on the ground," says Drury. "We'll set up in a patch of weeds or cedars, or in a brushy spot on a fence line. Large, round hay bales in and around a field make great blinds."

The key to any setup is thick background cover. You can get away with little or no brush in front, but you'd better cover your back, completely and with no air holes. A thick backdrop of sticks, brush, cedars or the like hides your silhouette and covers your moves as you draw your bow. That is the tough part.

"When a buck walks within 20 yards or so, you must stay cool and draw at just the right time," says Drury. "Pull and shoot either when the deer is looking directly away from you or back over his shoulder at another deer, or when his eyes are obscured by a tree or brush. It's pretty much the same as when shooting out of a tree. Only now a buck is right there at your level and larger than life. It's a pretty cool deal."

Hang with a buddy. Two hunters can set steps and stands easier, faster and quieter than one person can.

More Stand Tips:

➤ Sometimes, especially when cover is sparse in the treetops, it can pay to set an evening stand on a tree so that it faces a crop field or food plot. Deer will come from the woods and thickets to the rear, and the tree between you and them will provide good cover. If you shoot right-handed, set up where deer will pass within 30 yards to your left (vice versa for southpaws). You can draw and shoot with ease and little movement as a buck quarters past. Since you'll be facing downwind in this setup, shoot a deer quickly before he walks too far past and smells you.

➤ Say two deer trails run down a ridge or through a bottom. Which one will a buck take? Well, make him walk the one that runs closest to your stand. Drag a bunch of branches or a big deadfall into one trail to block it. When a buck comes along he'll skirt the obstacle and veer over to the trail you're covering.

➤ After hanging a stand, look around on the ground and remove any big logs or brushy tops that might block a buck from walking within 30 yards. If the cover is real tight, pull out your hand clipper and cut a small path 20 yards or so on the upwind side of your stand. When you come back to hunt in a few days you should see some fresh tracks in the new, clear trail.

➤ In the Midwest where many trees have lots of low limbs, the Drury boys use hang-on stands with stacking sticks or drilled-in bolts. But if you've got a lot of straight, limbless trees in your area, try a climber. You can pack one into a spot, run it 18 feet up a tree and hunt a buck in minutes. If the wind changes or you simply don't like that setup, you can climb back down and move quickly and easily. A climber is versatile and gives you an element of surprise that you can use to kill a big whitetail on occasion.

➤ You'll need a clipper and a folding saw to cut out spots for tree stands. A pole extension is a hassle to carry, but it makes your job a lot easier.

➤ It makes absolutely no sense to hang a stand in a spot where you can't shoot. You don't have to cut pulpwood, but trim at least three good shooting lanes to the upwind sides and front of your stand. Drag limbs and brushy tops away so deer won't smell your scent on them and so they won't block a buck's approach. After cutting, it's best to sneak out of a spot and rest it for a day or two before hunting.

➤ You stretch before a jog or a game of softball, right? So why not loosen up before hanging or climbing into a tree stand. At your truck, do some leg, arm and side-to-side torso stretches. The hike into a spot will further loosen you up. You'll hang and/or climb steps easier and safer.

➤ Try to hang a morning stand facing somewhere west, and an evening stand pointing toward the east. With the sun at your back, you'll have great visibility of the woods out front and below. You'll have the most shooting light at dawn and dusk. You'll be shaded nicely, lessening the odds that deer will look up and see you.

➤ Mark your stands not with gaudy flagging tape, but with "bright-eye" tacks or wraps. Flash a quick light on your markers as you sneak in or out at dawn or after dark and you won't stumble around looking for your stand and spooking deer.

➤ Go to Lowe's or Home Depot and buy three or four rubber-coated hardware hooks of various sizes. The hooks are a lot easier to start and screw into a tree than screw-in steps. Climb into a stand, sit down and screw the hooks within easy reach. Then organize and hang your bow, binocular, rattling horns and pack.

➤ Safety first! Never run a climbing stand up a tree or attempt to set steps and a fixed-position perch without wearing a climbing belt. Once 20 feet up and hunting, switch over to a four-point, full-body harness. The best harness I've worn is the Seat of the Pants model, which should be requisite gear for every bowhunter. It's available from Summit Tree Stands (*www.summitstands.com*) and also from Cabela's or Bass Pro Shops.

Chapter 4

Calling All Bucks

"Keep the faith and keep rattling, grunting or bleating until you strike a buck stoked to respond," says Will Primos. "It might happen any day, though you never know when."

I N A MINUTE, WE'LL LAY OUT SOME GREAT WAYS to trick bucks into bow range. But first let's get some preliminaries out of the way.

Despite all the hype and hoopla of the last decade, deer calling remains a dark and mysterious science. You need to keep in mind that rattling, grunting or bleating won't work every day, or even most days of the season. But keep whacking the horns and piping your calls, and one day out of the blue, you'll strike a chord with a buck. When it finally happens and an old 8-pointer rolls toward your stand with hackles up

and a demeanor that says, "I'm coming to kick butt!" you'll forget about all the down time.

Theoretically, rattling and calling can lure whitetails from September through January. But the tactics work best in the mating season, from the two-week scraping period of the pre-rut (Halloween till early November in most areas) through peak rut (November 10-20, give or take a few days) and into the initial days of post-breeding (late November/first week of December). Anytime during this span you're apt to encounter a buck on the hunt for the first or the last hot does. When things go

A big benefit of rattling from a tree stand is that you can look out and catch the flash of a buck that responds. Most deer circle in from somewhere downwind.

right and he likes what he hears, he'll commit to your grunts, love bleats or mock fights.

Calling can be effective anywhere in America, from Montana to New York to Alabama. It works best on a well-managed ground where the buck:doe ratio is near 1:1; where the age-structure of a herd is such that a good number of bucks $3\frac{1}{2}$ years of age and older roam; and where the pressure, especially with guns, is tightly controlled. On such a paradise, the rut is short and intense, and there is keen competition among the mature bucks for the sexual favors of the relatively few does. This is big, as the lightly pressured males are free to seek, chase and breed the gals at their leisure and during daylight hours, which makes them visible and vulnerable to calling archers.

All that is great, but out here in the real world most of us hunt private or public lands where the herds and the buck structures are a little to a lot out of kilter. Pressure may be moderate to army-like on your ground. All you can do is suck it up and hang tough.

A big benefit of ground ratting is mobility. Sneak downwind of a bedding area and whack the horns. If a buck doesn't show up in 30 minutes or so, slip to another cover and try again.

"Keep the faith and keep rattling, grunting or bleating until you finally hit that one buck that is pumped to respond," says Will Primos, headman at Primos Hunting Calls. "It might happen any day, though you never know when. Once you rattle or call in a buck or two, it gives you confidence to keep trying it more and more."

Rattling

On several occasions, Primos has seen and heard mature bucks fighting in mid-October, a full 2 months before the rut peaks on the properties he hunts in his home state of Mississippi. "I'm not talking about sparring," he notes. "Those bucks were flat-out trying to kill each other." So it goes to reason that you ought to play

Brad Farris spotted this buck's bleached tines bobbing in cover 200 yards away one November morning. He rattled and the big boy trotted right to his stand.

off that and start rattling from the outset of archery season, right? Well, not so fast.

"None of the early fights I've seen have ever attracted deer," notes the calling legend. "I've watched does and bucks in green fields look up at tangling bucks and then drop their heads and go right back to feeding." He believes that while some males fight to reaffirm their places in the buck hierarchy in early fall, most bucks already know their ranking and feel neither a testosterone surge nor the urgency to come watch a scrap.

Crack the horns too early, and in addition to not attracting deer, you might spook the hell out of a bunch of animals. One October afternoon not long ago I rattled at some does and bucks feeding in an alfalfa field a couple hundred yards from my bow stand. You would've thought I zapped 'em with a cattle prod! They didn't even bother to look. Every one of the deer threw up their flags and sprinted like gazelles for the nearest cover.

That incident and several others like it got me to wondering how many deer I've spooked like that over the years. Surely some does and bucks I could not see in the woods and thickets had heard my early mock fights and hauled butt in the opposite direction. So I've made the decision to leave my horns home in early to mid-October no matter where I'm hunting. That way I don't get the urge to rattle and spook the wits out of deer in the area.

"No doubt rattling is a timing deal," notes Primos, reaffirming what we said at the outset of this chapter. "Wherever we hunt, from Illinois to Montana to the Deep South, it works best for us that week before the peak of the rut." The pro keeps cracking horns right on through the peak and into the first week of the post-rut. "The technique produces more sporadic results in the middle to latter stages of the season, but still you never know when you'll strike a buck and reel him in."

When the time is right, either rattling blind or at a

I snapped this photo of Primos in a huge Texas oak years ago. Later that afternoon, he rattled up five bucks in the spot.

Try this unique rattling style: Hold one antler stationary and bang, grind and pop it with the other horn.

stands. This time Farris was shooting and Primos was running the camera. Once again, a couple of uneventful hours passed. Then with the sun up and pumping ivory light into the draw they spotted a buck sneaking back into the bedding area. Though the animal was a good 200 yards away, it was easy to see he was an old rascal, thick-bodied with saggy skin on his neck and face. His rack was heavy with short tines, and it reeked "mature."

Farris grabbed his horns and slammed them together. The deer stopped, turned, looked and kept going. "Hit 'em again," Primos whispered. Farris obliged, clicking and grinding the tines. The buck threw up his head, came on a trot and stopped smack below the tree. "Brad made a great shot and, as usual, ended up killing a better buck than I did on that trip," says Primos with a laugh.

The Mississippi pro agrees with those of us who say that sequence-wise there is no right or wrong way to rattle. But after watching and listening to many mature bucks fight, both in person from a stand and on the reams of tape his cameramen bring home each season, Primos has devised some sounds that he likes.

"When two big deer fight, they come together with a great smash of the antlers," he says. "Then as the bucks work their powerful necks and bodies and try to flip each other, there's mostly grinding, clicking and popping of tines. They might go 30 seconds without making much noise at all because the heavy deer are pressed and locked together so tightly. I keep all that in mind and try to mock it."

The pro has a unique style. "One other thing I've noticed is that real antlers with 200-pound bucks attached to them make heavy thudding sounds," Primos says. He has found that the best way to mimic those dull notes is to hold one antler in your left hand and keep it stationary and tight to your body. It never moves. Then bang, grind and pop on that antler with the horn in your right hand. In addition to realistic tones, you cut down on movements that could spook deer.

A great place to rattle in a rut-wild buck is on a hardwood ridge blazed with leg-size rubs and fresh scrapes. Ditto for a river or creek bottom or a series of draws with smoking sign. The thicker the cover and the more doe trails that crisscross an area the better. In such a hotspot, Primos and gang rattle mostly from tree stands because they're filming hunts for their "Truth About Hunting" DVDs and TV show, and elevated stands give them the

buck you see walking 60 to 200 yards out of bow range can be effective. A couple of recent magical days in Kansas with the Primos team illustrates why you ought to try it both ways.

It was November 8 and the rut was fixing to bust loose. Primos and his right-hand man Brad Farris were videoing in a two-stand set that overlooked a series of deep draws with short but thick cover. They'd hunted a couple of hours that morning and seen a few deer moving back toward the bedding cover, but nothing to write home about. "I'm gonna rattle," Will whispered.

Farris flicked on his camera. It's a good thing he did. A P&Y 8-pointer popped out of the brush, charged in and stopped 10 yards below their stands. "I don't ever remember a buck getting on top of me so fast," recalls Primos. "I barely had time to pick up my bow and draw, and it's a miracle Brad got the camera on him." Things worked out, and they killed the buck that came out of nowhere.

Two mornings later they went back to the same

I grunt sharply to every buck I see cruising out of bow range. Almost every deer that hears it stops and looks. Sometimes a big boy turns my way and things get interesting.

After a rattling volley lay down your horns and do a little grunting in hopes of reeling a buck close. Have your bow close and ready.

best visibility of incoming bucks.

"But we've also had some fantastic hunts on the ground," he notes. "You can crack the horns and *bam*, a big deer can run in and be all up in your face in a hurry. Plus, if you don't bring in a buck at one spot, you can slip easily and quietly another 200 yards into the wind and try it again and again."

When rattling from ground zero, Primos advises this trick: "Have a buddy set up 20 to 50 yards behind you and whack and grind the horns. Let him do all the rattling and you concentrate on the shooting. If a buck comes in and focuses his attention on the rattler, it makes it a lot easier for you to turn, draw and fire an arrow."

The final piece in the set-up puzzle "is to make a buck hunt you," says the Mississippi game call maker. "Choose a rattling spot close to some type of visual obstruction, like a creek bank, downed treetop or cane thicket. If you set up in open woods and rattle, a buck will look your way, but he won't see another deer over there. He might be leery to come. But if you can make a buck think he needs to look behind a treetop or bank or inside a thicket, you'll have a much better opportunity to pull him close, draw your bow and make the shot."

"If I had to give up all my calls but one, I'd hang on to my bleat," says Primos, shown here with one of his CAN calls.

Grunting

One afternoon years ago, scouting a property along the Mississippi River in early October, Primos found a couple of persimmon trees starting to drop their pulpy fruits. The trees were 100 yards apart, and his dilemma was to decide which one to hunt. He flipped a coin, chose the winning tree and hung a stand nearby.

Later that evening, two does walked beneath the *other* tree and began gobbling the sweet fruits. For kicks, Primos raised his call and uttered one short, soft grunt. Both does looked up and went back to eating. He grunted once more, and the lead doe looked up again, turned, marched to the persimmon tree 30 yards from his stand and went back to feeding. Primos didn't shoot a deer that night, but he learned a lot. "It drove home just how effective contact grunts can be early in the season. It made me start grunting quite a bit more in October than I usually did. Since then, I can't tell you how many does and bucks I've called in early over the years."

To make those contact grunts, huff air into a tube to say *ecc, ecc* or *urk, urk.* On stand in the morning or the afternoon, string together a few soft grunts every 15, 30 or 60 minutes, whatever feels right at the time. The calls

are non-threatening and should never spook a deer. To the contrary, you might reel in an animal looking for company.

As October flies by and the rut approaches, bucks become more vocal and brazen. So should you. The day you see big, musky scrapes and more shredded rubs pop up in the woods, crank it up and blow "aggression" or "tending grunts." Your throaty, deep-pitched calls should sound like *urrrp, urrrp, urrrp* or *urrrg, urrrg, urrrg.* Five- to 10-second sequences are most realistic, but grunt shorter or longer if you like.

"I've heard rutting bucks make all sorts of long, loud, wild sounds," notes Primos. "When you grunt in the rut, make calls that are emotionally charged and try to impart a sense of urgency." His thinking is that a horny buck may come to what he perceives to be a rival chasing or tending a hot doe, or an interloper prowling around and cruising for a bruising.

Like rattling, blind grunting can be effective. Every season you hear tell of bowhunters sitting on stand and blowing long and loud on their calls. All at once they look over and there stands a drooling, glassy-eyed, 150- to 170-class buck! The lesson: Carry a tube every day in

the rut and don't be afraid to use it!

Grunting can work even better when you see a buck cruising out of bow range. "Say you spot a big deer cresting a ridge or slipping down a draw 80 yards away," says Primos. "If he's going the other way, you'd be crazy not to call to him. If he hears you, most of the time he'll at least stop and look."

Typically a buck will stop, look and continue on his merry way. Well, don't just sit there, grunt some more, louder and sharper! You might also ease up your rattling horns and do a little cracking and grinding. A combo of grunting and rattling has tricked many a good buck.

Once the rut is over in December, you need to read the mood and body language of each deer that cruises within view of your stand. "Some bucks are still wired and looking for does, and they'll come to aggressive grunts," notes Primos. "But most deer are skinny, worn out and wary. To call in a buck like that, you need to tone way down. Go back to blowing contact grunts to sound like deer taking it easy and feeding."

Bleating

One afternoon about 10 years ago, Primos was hunting and filming at Willow Point Island, a popular archery-only lodge located near Vicksburg, Mississippi. A doe walked out into a food plot 75 yards away and started bleating softly, *mea, mea, mea*. Five bucks jogged in and started feeding alongside her. When the gal finished her meal, she bleated once more and walked back into the woods. The bucks dutifully followed.

"They were little guys, spikes and 4-pointers, but it was wild how they locked in on those bleats," recalls Primos. "I had heard does bleat before, but that was the first time I witnessed just how powerful the vocalization is. It gave me the confidence to start bleating more and more. Now if you told me I had to give up all my calls except one, I'd hang on to my bleat."

Doe and domestic sheep bleats sound similar, though deer bleats don't have quite the same wavering quality. Each bleat lasts 1 to 2 seconds and sounds like *mea* or *waa*, depending on how you interpret the sound. In early fall, it never hurts to bleat a few times from your stand every 30 minutes or so, especially when you're set up en route to a food plot, acorn tree or other feeding area. A deer or two might veer over for a look. If you spot a buck out of bow range and walking away from you, bleat a few times to stop the deer and hold him in the area. Bleating might actually be better for this job than grunting "because I've noticed that some deer seem to hear bleats farther away than they hear grunts," notes Primos. "Blow a bleat call fairly hard and you get notes with a sharp, high pitch."

During the rut, especially those two or three wild days just before the mature does pop into heat, Primos relies heavily on the "estrus bleat." In fact, it has become one of his favorite calls. He uses his company's cylindrical CAN, which works on the same principle as the old turnover toy that sounded like a mooing cow. Simply turn the CAN over and over in your hand to make sassy, drawn-out *meaaaa, meaaaa, meaaas*. "A doe on the brink of estrus is stressed out and fussy, and I think she's telling any buck that will listen that she's just about ready to breed," explains the Mississippi pro.

Primos has a trove of stories about how estrus bleating can bring a mega buck running. One of my favorites is from a recent hunt of his in Kansas. One morning, he spotted an old, thick-bodied P&Y animal dogging a doe back into a bedding area. The deer were 150 yards out and going away, so he had to get down on his CAN. He turned it over and over and filled the air with loud, fussy bleats. Finally, the doe heard the ruckus and stopped and looked. He kept working his CAN. The doe broke and trotted straight for his stand. "Guess who was right behind her?" asks Primos, smiling as he recalled zipping an arrow through the buck's lungs. "People say you can't rattle or grunt a buck off a hot doe, and they're right. So why not bleat in a doe and let her bring a buck along?"

Sometimes when he's sitting in a tree stand with no deer in sight, Primos floats a series of sassy bleats and backs 'em up with an aggravated doe snort or two. "It's not those foot-stamping danger snorts, but more of a general blowing or wheezing that deer make," he explains. "If a doe is not ready to breed, maybe a day or two off, she'll blow at a buck. Other bucks listen for that, and sometimes one will run in to check it out." Other days, in an effort to make something good happen, the call maker mimics a breeding scenario by uttering fussy bleats followed by loud, deep-pitched tending grunts.

One cool, clear November morning a few years ago in Illinois, Primos hung in a tree stand on a ridge blazed with big rubs and smoking scrapes. Things had been slow, so he decided to get pro-active. For 15 minutes he went through his entire repertoire. He worked his CAN and followed the beats with long, loud grunts. He cracked and ground his horns and grunted some more like a market hog. He laid down his tools, picked up his bow and waited.

Minutes later he heard an unmistakable crunching in the leaves – the stiff-legged gait of a rutting buck! He turned his head and caught the flash of antlers in the sun. The thick, 160-inch monster was coming on a string and looking hard. Was it the rattles, grunts or bleats that attracted him?

"Who knows and who cares?" bellows Primos with a grin. "All I know is that I killed that great deer at 20 steps by mixing it up and sounding like deer doing their thing. That's what calling is really all about, especially in the rut."

Simply turn a CAN call over and over to fill the woods with sexy doe bleats. Again, have your bow ready in case a horny buck gallops in.

Calling Tips:

➤ Rattle and/or call where deer are most apt to hear you – near feeding areas in the afternoon, near bedding thickets in the morning and in doe funnels anytime of day during the rut. It's worth trying in any spot littered with fresh tracks and other buck sign.

➤ Grunt or bleat loudly enough for deer to hear you, especially on windy days. "Most hunters are tentative and call too softly," notes Primos. "Make a buck hear you 100 yards or farther away."

➤ Don't sit on stand and grunt in a monotone. Put some life into your calls by varying the volume and excitability of the notes, especially during the rut.

Don't be afraid to bear down on a call, especially if it's windy. You've got to make bucks hear you.

➤ When rattling in the rut, get really nasty and set out some buck urine or tarsal. Set scent wicks not only out front of your stand but also 50 yards or so to either side of it. If a buck circles downwind of your mock fight, as a big deer is apt to do, he might hit one of your scent-posts and come in off to the side before he gets dead downwind and smells you.

Vary the volume and length of your grunts to put life into your routine.

➤ Mossy Oak bags with plastic or wooden dowels inside are convenient to carry and use in a tree stand. On the downside, they don't produce a lot of volume. Most of the time, it's better to bang a large set of sheds or synthetic antlers to reach out and touch a buck (Primos' molded Fighting Horns work great).

➤ Don't rattle or call when a buck is close and looking in your direction. He might see you move or, more likely, he'll look over there and see no deer. He'll get wise and hang up.

➤ Stop grunting when a buck locks in and moves your way. Let him come and get ready to draw and shoot. Call again only if the deer loses interest and veers off.

➤ A rut-crazy buck might charge across a crop field or grassland to check out rattles or guttural grunts (it happens all the time down in Texas), but in other regions, you're better off setting up in "broken" cover where a big buck feels most comfortable working in through trees and thickets.

Use either sheds or synthetic horns. Sometimes a few clicks or grinds are all it takes.

➤ Say you know a good buck is working a ridge and adjacent creek bottom. Well, opt for the high ground. Up on the ridge, the wind and thermals are more predictable, so there's less chance the buck will smell a rat if he comes to your calls. Also, the higher you hunt, the easier it is for deer to hear your calls.

➤ Sneak quietly into an area and set up with the wind in your face. But watch your sides and back. Mature bucks often circle into rattling or grunting from downwind. To keep that from happening, try to sit with a river, steep slope or similar "buck block" behind you. A big deer might try to circle, but he'll be forced to angle in from the side or front.

➤ Put the rising or setting sun at your back. If a buck comes in, you'll easily pick up the flash of his antlers or hide. And it will be tough for him to see you rattling or raising a grunt tube.

➤ During peak rut, cover lots of country after sunup and look for a big 8- or 10-pointer chasing a doe or nudging one back into a small cover. When the deer disappear into a thicket or patch of timber, make your move. Hide behind terrain and foliage and sneak quietly to the first downwind edge of the cover where the big boy is having his fun only a couple hundred yards away. Set up in a makeshift ground blind where you can see well out front and off to the sides. Break out your horns and rattle like hell for a minute or two to mimic a couple of intruders. Pick up your bow and get ready. The wild-eyed buck might be in your face before you know it! But give it 30 minutes. The deer might circle in slowly or a satellite buck that heard your racket might crash your party.

47

Chapter 5

October Bucks

WHEN THE CALENDAR FLIPS TO OCTOBER **1,** opening day in many states, the hormones of the bucks are not yet raging like those of teenagers on prom night. Many males are still in bachelor clubs, keeping their distance from the fairer sex. But as the air grows crisper, the days shorter and the leaves a brighter shade of gold and red, big deer morph from docile critters (the first two weeks of the month) to rubbing, scraping fiends (around the 20th) to wild-eyed, sex-starved beasts (around Halloween). This progression is as predictable as it is swift each fall. Tailor your archery strategies to each specific phase of the pre-rut to take full advantage of a buck's rapidly changing behavior. To help you do that, I enlisted the help of legendary whitetail hunter David Hale of Cadiz, Kentucky.

October 1-15

Consider some things that will drive your strategy this week and next:

- Whitetails stick to their summer bed-to-feed routines. Traveling alone, in pairs or in small bachelor gangs, mature bucks creep along trails and funnels, moving "lazily and mostly at dusk and night," says Hale.
- Many old bucks stay visible until around the 10th of the month in crop fields, cutovers, power-line cuts and other openings like they were back in August and September. Glass *a lot* and pattern the deer.
- The hotter it is, the slower bucks move. If you were wearing a full-length winter fur coat, you wouldn't jog down a sidewalk on a 60- or 70-degree afternoon now would you? It might take a shooter an hour to cover 100 or 200 yards. "Besides, a big deer is lazy by nature, and that is easy to see in early October," points out Hale.
- Mature deer don't travel far. If you spot a big 8- or 10-pointer, he'll almost certainly live close by for the next few weeks. "Heck, he might stay within 500 acres or so all month or all season," adds Hale.
- October deer are touchy, but since we haven't hunted them for 10 months, their guard is a little down. Find and pattern a Pope & Young animal, go into stealth mode, sneak into a spot undetected and you've got one of your best chances of the year to score big.

David Hale waits till November to rattle, but he grunts at every October buck he spots from a stand.

If it's hot and dry in early October, try watching a waterhole near feed. Hale arrowed this brute from a stand he'd hung between the pond and the oak ridge in the background.

Glass frequently as you approach a stand in early afternoon. Your goal is to sneak in and set up without busting one animal.

you can cover *both* food sources and your odds shoot way up.

The whole enchilada is predicated on your having glassed and patterned at least one or two shooters in a field or timber opening over the summer, so I hope you did your homework. Anyway, one day around lunchtime put the wind in your face and go investigate major deer trails that lead out of a field and back into the surrounding timber. A good run might look like a cattle path this time of year since so many does and fawns use it.

You might be able to set up hard on a field edge and shoot a good buck. But remember, if the edge is long and relatively straight, a buck might pop out into the feeding area 50 to 100 yards or more to one side of your perch. For the bowhunter, he might as well be a mile away!

To tighten things up, Hale looks for something that will funnel deer out of the woods and into the crops. "A big old buck loves to walk along or through cover for as far as he can. Look for a weed ditch, brushy fencerow or head of timber that juts out into a field. Any little bit of cover that sticks out into the crops is a good spot for a tree stand."

In many regions of the country, once bow season has been on for a few days, a big deer won't walk out into an agricultural field until right at dusk or after dark. To get a shot at him in the last wisps of light, you'll have to hunt a ways back in the surrounding

Hunting is best in the afternoons tight to where bucks come to eat like hogs and to fatten up in anticipation of the rut. A field of alfalfa, corn or clover, or a flat or ridge with falling acorns is best. Find a spot where timber. When probing back and looking for a good setup, use your head and don't walk on a deer trail. Parallel it on the downwind side. No matter how well the terrain and foliage hide your moves, *do not* penetrate

Some of the best October hunting occurs in river bottoms across the country. Whitetails rest in thickets near the water and move out to nearby crop fields in the afternoons. If you have access to this type of habitat, hunt it!

more than 100 yards. "If you push any deeper into the woods, you're apt to bust a bunch of deer that will scatter like quail," says Hale. "Many does and bucks bed tight to the feed in early fall."

At some point 50 to 100 yards off a field, a main trail should splinter into two or three feeder paths. Deer drop off ridges and walk up out of draws, coming from all directions in the woods before funneling into a feeding area. Stop right there—an intersection is a great spot!

Test the wind. Later that afternoon, or tomorrow or on the third day when you come back with your bow, the breeze must blow somewhere back toward the field before you can even think of hunting your new great spot. If it seems that will be the case, hang a tree stand within 30 yards of the trail junction. If you use a climber, you might actually shinny up 20 feet and hunt right then and there that afternoon. But if you wrestle with a fixed-position stand, you can't help but rattle a chain or bang a buckle, and you'll lay down a pool of scent. Any deer bedded nearby might hear or smell a rat, so rest the stand for a day or two.

When you do sneak back in to hunt, keep your eyes open, especially those last dingy minutes of dusk. Alone or with a buddy or two, a bruiser might lollygag on one of those trails, planning to arrive at the field behind you at dark. Shoot straight and cut him off at the pass.

"To make the set even stronger, look and listen for acorns falling within 25 to 50 yards or so of a trail junction," notes Hale. "But again, don't press too far back in the woods while scouting or you'll ruin a good thing. If you find fresh acorns, look for a flurry of rubs, sign that a buck or two or maybe even a bachelor club is gorging there. Hang a stand tight to the mast, or along a nearby trail where the wind is better. You've got a great opportunity."

October 16-23

You live for the first cold front of October. That initial blast of cool, clear air makes the deer feel better, just like it puts a skip in your step. Old bucks start to move more. They lay down sign and start to nudge does around.

Some rain followed by a shocking drop of 20 to 40 degrees can kick the whitetail activity up a notch. But

Bucks have rubbed this tree for years—note the healed and fresh scars—so you know it's in a spot that gets a good amount of deer traffic.

downwind of a trail blazed with shiny, bark-shredded rubs. That's quite possibly the work of a heavy-racked hawg. Studies have shown that in an area where the age structure of the bucks is good, deer 3½ years of age and older lay down most of the first big rut sign.

"Rubs and especially rub lines can be tough to find early when the brush is thick and the leaves are still on the trees," says Hale. "But snoop around and do the best you can. Scout for clusters of big, shiny rubs. They're easiest to find. Then look out from those for smaller rubs that show a buck's travel route between his bedding area and food sources."

If you get lucky and find a mother lode of fresh rubs, read the terrain, play the wind and hang a bow stand in the vicinity. "You'll be somewhere inside a buck's core area," notes Hale, "and you can't ask for much more than that."

Also, now is the time to start looking for what the Kentucky pro calls "random" scrapes. "You'll often find these first scrapes scattered on a ridge or in a bottom and mixed in among the rubbed trees. I believe a buck is mostly venting pent-up energy, and he usually won't come back to check the scrapes. But it's a good sign of a good buck working the area."

With rubs and random scrapes in mind, hang a tree stand where you can see out into a nearby food plot, or across an oak flat, ridge or bottom. "Bucks are starting to feel the rut, but they're still patternable deep into October," notes Hale. "They'll continue to travel in and through the same areas where you find fresh sign. It's a great time to sit back, observe and get a good inventory of the bucks in your area."

If a big deer walks beneath your observation post one afternoon, thank your luck and take him. If you spy Mr. Big working the next ridge or cutting out into a field 100 yards away, sit tight in the stand. "But if you spot the buck doing the same thing two or three afternoons in a row, sneak over there and hang another stand for a surprise ambush," says Hale.

October 24-31

A research project in the late 1990s monitored the scraping behavior of whitetails on a well-managed and smartly hunted property in northern Georgia. It was one of the best and most practical studies I have ever seen on scraping, and one of the biologist's findings really

then so can a subtle cooling off of 10 degrees or so. "More so than the temperature drop, I believe the falling barometer associated with a front is what makes bucks get up and move," says Hale. "Watch your barometric pressure. Hunt the afternoons when it starts going down."

The Kentucky pro loves to bowhunt the day before a northerly or westerly front rolls in. The one or two high-pressure days after a front blows through are also good, though you'll often have to deal with moderate to high winds. But you can handle it because bucks should move earlier and harder to food sources.

Keep watching major trails into the feed. Only now, begin to tweak your setup in a couple of ways. Hunt

You might find pawings on a ridge or bottom in mid-October. "Bucks won't come back to work those scrapes, but they tell you deer are working the area," notes Hale.

From Halloween on, Hale hangs tough on stand each morning. He watches for a buck trying to scare up a hot doe up until 11:00 a.m. or so. Late mornings can be great this time of year!

for a ridge, strip of timber or similar funnel that connects a thicket or old weed field with a nearby grain field or oak flat where you've been spotting a lot of does," says Hale. "The best funnel to hunt will have a couple of big doe trails, a bunch of fresh scrapes and, best of all, some big rubs." The pro points out that a spindly 6-pointer or a 150-inch brute might have dug those scrapes, but generally only a deer with a powerful neck and a big rack mauls trees as thick as your calf.

To catch a shooter on a ridge or in a draw in the last gray light, hang a bow stand 50 to 100 yards *off the feed and back toward a bedding cover.* If you find a long line of scrapes and figure Mossy Horns is traveling a really long ways between bed and feed, probe 50 to 100 yards deeper into the woods. The bucks are more aggressive now. You should be too.

When you find a midway point in a funnel, you've still got a big dilemma: Set your stand tight to a doe trail or scrape line, or a far piece downwind of it? I have sat and watched many good bucks prowl down a doe trail like they owned it; some of the deer stopped to maul trees and rip scrapes. I have also sat and watched giants loop through cover 50 to 100 yards downwind of scrapes, scent-checking them before circling up to the trail proper.

I figure it's best, at least initially, to set up 75 to 100 yards downwind of a trail or scrapes rather than smack on top of them. Hale agrees. "That way a buck won't come in and see or smell you from the git-go," says the pro. "And who knows, he might even circle in and give you a shot. But if not, it's no big deal. If you spot a buck on a trail or scrape line 100 yards away a couple of evenings in a row, you can always move your stand in tighter on the third day and try to get him."

Up until now, the best bowhunting has been in the afternoons. But the deeper into October you go, the better the mornings get. If on or around Halloween morning you can play the wind and slip into a hollow or onto a ridge blazed with hot sign, go for it. Sneak to your stand in the pitch dark, climb up, nock an arrow and pull on your mask. "If it's cool, say in the 20s or 30s, there's a good chance you'll spot a buck walking around with his nose down, trying to scare up a doe," notes Hale. "Watch for him right on up until 11:00 a.m. or so. Midmornings can be great."

If you don't see the big fella, don't sweat it. There's always next month when the rut really rocks.

jumped out at me. The researchers found that some of the heaviest scraping in October occurs just after dusk each day. I believe you can play off that and increase your scrape-hunting success dramatically.

As bucks get up and paw to blow off weeks of sexual frustration, they lay down a lot of sign near their bedding covers. Also, they blaze rubs and scrapes en route to food sources where they'll scent-check does. "Look

The second week of October one year, deer vanished from Hale's food plots. He snuck onto an oak ridge where the animals had moved to feed on acorns and killed this buck.

October Timeline

To take full advantage of a buck's changing behaviors, keep these key dates in mind. Dates are approximate for central and northern states.

October 1: Some summer bachelor groups of three to six bucks begin to break up; other bucks will still travel in pairs or threes for the next two weeks. It is not uncommon to spot a giant deer traveling with one or more immature, spindly-racked bucks.

October 5: Here's one from the "I bet you didn't know this" file: Around this time, "licking sticks" start popping up in the woods, according to Leonard Lee Rue III, the first whitetail authority to record the sign. A licking stick is a 1-inch sapling snapped off 3 feet up; a buck strips bark off the top as he rubs on scent and licks it. "These lesser-known signposts are not left along trails but seem to be made as the bucks wander through the forest gathering acorns," Rue writes in *Way of the Whitetail* (Voyageur Press, 2000). "They are usually overlooked by most hunters—but not by the deer. Licking sticks draw deer like iron filings to a magnet." Start scouting for them.

October 8: Georgia researchers found that bucks begin working overhead lick branches and urinating at scrape sites now, but the full-blown pawing has yet to begin.

October 9: Last acorns fall in many regions, giving does and bucks one last chance to gorge. Key on that last mast, and you're sure to see deer.

October 15: Bucks necks begin to swell. Some scientists say the testosterone levels rise faster in 3- to 5-year-old bucks than in 1- to 2-year-olds, causing the old boys to lay down sign earlier. While mature deer have been rubbing since late August and September, they

Pre-Rut Tips:

➤ In early to mid-October, hang at least three tree stands near food sources that you can hunt on different winds, from southeast to northwest. In addition to crops and acorns, look for beechnuts, apples, persimmons or other mast deer might hit.

➤ Access stands from the food-source side and downwind each afternoon. Creep in behind cover and terrain; try not to crack a stick, squeak a wire fence, etc.

➤ Note ridges and draws where you find the most acorns. That's where you'll find a ton of rubs and scrapes in a few weeks.

➤ On a warm, still October evening, thermals can be killer, in a bad way. Try to set up on the low side of a ridge or field. When the air cools and sinks toward dark, hopefully your scent will flow down and away from where deer walk.

Shh! Going to your stand, don't squeal a fence or snap a stick.

➤ Four big tracks with a monster standing in them are your best sign in early October. If you hunt a few days but can't get onto a good

deer, sacrifice one or two evenings and mornings to scout. Glass like crazy, find a buck, pin down where he enters and leaves a feeding area and move in for a quick strike.

➤ Go to *www.weather.com*, click on "Hourly Forecast" and check out the precipitation and wind data. Use that information to plan one or two day's worth of hunting around an October cold front, or anytime of the season for that matter. Keep checking the website. The hourly wind directions and speeds get more accurate the closer you get to hunting time.

➤ On a windy afternoon on the backside of a front, you won't spot many deer in fields or on the tops of ridges. Choose a stand in a sheltered ditch, hollow or creek bottom that links a feeding and bedding area.

➤ As you walk to and from your stands, note ridges, draws and edges where new rubs and scrapes pop up. Cross-reference the sign on

really begin to maul trees and mark their core areas now. Look for fresh rubs, the bigger the better.

October 16: Kicked out by their mamas, many 1½-year-old bucks begin dispersing miles to new core areas. These are the small-racked "floaters" you see wandering the woods—the ones you ought to pass up and let grow another year.

October 18: Last of the bachelor clubs split. Solitary old bucks become increasingly ornery and aggressive, though they stick to their core areas and move mostly at night.

October 23: The hard-core digging begins. Multiple bucks may paw and rub-urinate at the same

scrapes, mostly at night. Big deer gradually begin to expand their ranges to scent-check does, but if your property has lots of quality feed and hence a good number of does, most bucks will hang tight.

October 25: Pumped with testosterone, bucks should move well at dusk and dawn, especially in years when a dark moon overlaps this week. Old bucks can no longer suppress the young males, which jump hooves first into the rubbing/scraping ritual.

Halloween: Bucks prowl hard, noses to the ground and grunting, for the first estrous does, as the seeking phase of the rut begins. If two big rivals cross paths near a doe feeding or bedding area, one hell of a fight might break out.

an aerial photograph and start predicting where the heavy rutting action will happen over the next three weeks.

➤ Look for five, 10 or more rubs on a ridge. If the trees are thrashed on the uphill side, the buck walked down the ridge toward feed or his bed as he blazed the sign. If the trees are marked on the downhill side, the buck walked up the ridge. "Try hanging a trail camera close to the rubs," says Hale. "You might photograph and time a big deer moving from bed to feed. The great thing about October is that bucks are still patternable."

➤ Hunt as many mornings as you can in late October. Cool temps combined with a dark moon (if you've got one) will cause bucks to move well at dawn.

➤ Georgia biologists have found that four or five bucks and some does might mill around one set of scrapes while scrapes 150 yards away go stale. If you sit two days without spotting many deer, stop wasting your time. Move your stand to a nearby ridge or draw where scrapes are bigger and fresher.

➤ It couldn't hurt to douse a scrape near your stand with tarsal every day in late October. Your "intruder" scent might attract a prowling buck.

When bow season opens, Hale blows soft contact grunts. As October progresses and the rut draws closer, he cranks up the volume and intensity of his calls.

57

Chapter 6

Bowhunting the Rut

IF YOU HEED THE ADVICE IN THE PRECEDING CHAP-
TER, there's a good chance you'll tag out in
October. But some seasons you won't be so
lucky … or you'll sail an arrow over a big
deer's spine one afternoon … or maybe you
will score early, but a second archery permit in your
home state or a state next door burns a hole in your
pocket. Well, read on. Harold Knight, one of the top
whitetail gurus in America, helps out with some great
strategies for the peak of the rut, those wild and turbu-
lent weeks when you really want to be out in the woods
anyway. And just in case your hunt for a giant whitetail
goes down to the wire, we offer one last plan for
Thanksgiving week.

Keep in mind that the strategies outlined here are
geared to the November rut in states north of the 35th
parallel. If you live or hunt in the Deep South, the tactics will certainly work, but you'll need to adjust your
timetable to coincide with the normal rut dates in your
area.

November 1-16

For five thrilling minutes, I watched the 10-pointer
fling dirt, pee and mangle an overhead limb. When the
morning hunt was over, I yanked my stand and crept
over to the ridge where I had glassed the rutting giant.
Which scrape had he worked? The placed looked like a
hog lot, and the stench of tarsal hung in the air. Who
cared? I re-hung my perch in the middle of it all and
snuck away.

The 160-incher loped down the ridge the next
morning, hot after a doe he had hooked up with
overnight. No shot, but my bummer was short-lived.
Thirty minutes later, a barrel-chested 8-pointer wan-

dered by, his mind in a daze and his nose to the ground,
and I nailed him with a 2213 tipped with a three-blade
broadhead.

You can dawdle away your precious hunting time in
a so-so stand, or you can pick up like I did and go kill
a buck. The first two weeks of November are the time to
go for it. Bucks are getting sky high on testosterone, but
most of them still stick to some semblance of a pattern.
They cruise the same ridges, draws and thickets for does,
and bed in roughly the same spots. Even if you spot a
monster chasing a gal, chances are he won't run her far.
The deer will probably loop round and round the same
50- to 100-acre patch of brush or timber.

After spotting an eye-popping rack, sneak in and
check things out. If a ridge or draw is laced with smoking scrapes and shredded rubs, Mr. Big should be
back—maybe later that afternoon, or tomorrow morning
or the third day. There's a bonus. While most bucks are
still homebodies this week, some have gone on the lam,
wandering out of their core areas in search of the first
hot does. A vagabond will home in on a ridge or draw
where he sees and smells other rutting deer. That's
where you need to be.

"That is a great story and some fine advice," says
Knight. "I'll add that when big, fresh buck sign pops up
in a hot-looking spot, don't think twice about moving in
and hanging a bow stand smack on top of a doe trail
where the wind is right. If you sit long enough with fresh
sign all around you, a big deer should come trolling
down that trail looking for a doe sooner or later."

*Harold Knight killed this buck on a scrape-laced ridge near a
food plot. "Where the does go to eat, the bucks follow," he says,
"and they often walk on or near a line of scrapes."*

Say two mornings in a row you spot a big 8-pointer running a ridge or scraping on a field edge 200 yards away. Pull your stand, sneak over and re-hang it in a tree in the middle of the action. Your third day might be a charm.

Knight also has no qualms about going in and setting up tight to a scrape line that runs, say, 150 yards out from a thicket and toward a field or oak ridge where a bunch of does feed. "In early November, food is still a big deal because it drives the movement of does mostly in the afternoons, but also some in the mornings. Where the does go, the bucks will follow, and they'll often walk on or near a line of hot scrapes."

The Kentucky pro offers some final thoughts on bowhunting scrapes. "I key on big scrapes with licking branches way back in the woods, or at least scrapes that are surrounded by heavy cover. The more a big deer feels hidden, the more comfortable he feels traveling and scraping. I watch those scrapes early in the morning and right up until noon or so as well. A lot of times an old buck will search for does all night, bed down at first light and get up later in the morning to check his scrapes. Man, David and I have shot some great bucks around scrapes between ten a.m. and lunchtime."

Knight has found over the years that scrape hunting is most productive during a dark moon phase. New moon, first-quarter or last-quarter, it doesn't seem to matter. "Anytime the moon is fully or partially dark in early to mid-November, you're apt to catch a buck checking his scrapes, or at least cruising through an area where he lays down a lot of sign."

November 16-23

While this is the best week to pack a gun in many regions, it is the toughest week to archery hunt. With so much stuff going on in the woods, it's hard to decide how and where to set up. The good news is that the rut is full-bore in many places. You might spot a shooter wandering aimlessly around with his nose to the ground … or dogging a doe … or chasing one full-tilt across a field or creek bottom.

Then again, you might not see squat, because many of the big boys have turned nocturnal as vampires and are rutting at night. To boot, they're holed up and servicing estrous does in thickets.

Of course, you might see or hear deer running wildly over hill and dale. Gun season is on in many areas; other guys kill some bucks and scare the daylights out of many more. All things considered, it's probably best

The Knight and Hale team has dragged out many a P-&-Y buck during the rut. One of their top tactics is to watch big, dank scrapes deep in the woods from 9:00 a.m. till noon.

The bigger the scrape the bigger the buck—right? Not necessarily. But if you find leg-size rubs near 4-foot scrapes, you can figure a stud worked there.

to go find a funnel and sit in it.

Study an aerial map and scout for a hidden spot where two or three hogback ridges and draws converge and peter out, maybe in a creek or river bottom. "The thicker the cover the better," points out Knight. "And look for heavy trails that run off the ridges and drop down into the hollows and bottoms where does feed and bed. The hunt-the-does strategy applies now."

A hardwood ridge laced with heavy brush and second growth is an awesome spot to hang a bow stand and watch for a buck lollygagging around or chasing a doe. Hunt as high as the terrain and cover allow. You'll see well, and the wind and thermals should be fairly steady up there.

One of Knight's favorite places for an archery stand is on the edge of a weed field or a regenerating clear-cut. "Bucks love head-high cover, but during the rut they also want to be able to see well, and be seen by does. A weed field or clear-cut offers some security, but it also gives the deer visibility. It's a great spot to kill a buck."

Wherever you hunt, get on post early each morning

and hunt long and hard till midday. If you can hack it, sit all day. Key on every doe you see, especially the big, old loners. "A mature doe all by herself is probably ready to breed, and she might even be looking for a buck. Watch her close and watch where she goes. A buck is gonna be on her tail real soon."

As you pass the hours on stand, keep your edge the best you can. Watch for a shooter popping over a ridge, shortcutting from one draw to the next as he seeks a girl friend. Glass into thickets for a bedded doe; look around her for a wide-eyed mate. He might stand up anytime and give you a good look at his rack. Look and listen for deer pushed by other hunters on neighboring lands. They're apt to roll in over a ridge and dive into a draw cover you're watching.

"You never know what might happen," says Knight with a chuckle. "But I know one thing, if you hunt a good stand hard during the peak week you *will* see a lot of deer, and maybe one with a huge rack. Best of all, you'll have a lot of fun."

November 24-30

Funny how things come full circle. In late October, you looked for hogbacks, draws, strips of timber and bottoms where bucks scraped like fiends as they prowled toward food sources and scent-checked for the first estrous does. Well now, exactly one month later, go back and check those spots again in hopes of running across an old 8- or 10-pointer cruising for the last hot gals. There is both scientific evidence and pro-hunter advice for doing so.

An excellent University of Georgia study a few years ago found that when bucks start chasing and breeding does in mid-November, they virtually stop digging and tending scrapes. "I definitely agree with that," says Knight. "The hottest scrapes can go cold overnight."

The study went on to point out that along about November 20, some bucks 2½ years of age and older go back to checking old, closed scrapes in their home core areas, and they keep it up through the first week of December. Apparently, the prospect of hooking up with one last doe before it's all over for another year is too much for the boys to resist.

"Late in November, I go back to my favorite pre-rut spots, places where I found a lot of sign and spotted bucks earlier in the season, and I check out the scrapes again," adds Knight. "If they're freshly worked and opened up, I know at least one big deer is back in the area, searching for the last does. I'll go back and hunt a stand I already have hung in the area, or I'll put up one. By the way, the day after a rain or snow is a great time to check scrapes. It's quiet walking in the woods, and it's easy to see if a scrape was just reopened."

There are a couple of caveats to this strategy. Some bucks never return to their scrapes—they were shot last week or the week before by either bow or gun hunters. And the survivors are wired and nocturnal now. You won't see nearly as many bucks cruising around as you did back in late October. But it only takes one to make your bow season!

Also, it's Thanksgiving, one of the most heavily hunted weeks of the year. "You need to poke around and hopefully find a thick little spot where nobody is gun hunting," says Knight. That might be a ridge near a cornfield you bowhunted back in October, or a scraped-

Check scrapes again in late November. If they've been reopened, you can surmise a buck is back, looking for a last hot doe.

up draw where you moved in on a buck the first week of this month. Keep your options open.

In the mornings, set up midway in a funnel, 50 to 100 yards off a food source and back toward thick bedding cover. "A dark moon is best for buck movement in and around thickets at first light," says Knight.

In the afternoons, sneak out to a grain field, clear-cut or oak flat—anywhere there's still a little feed—and hang a stand or hide in a ground blind on an edge where the wind is right. Bucks and does are tired, thin and hungry now. They'll hit the feed, maybe before dark if it's real cold and if the pressure is not too hot and heavy. You might finally tag Mr. Big.

Mossy Oak's Toxey Haas has two passions: growing and hunting mature bucks.

November Timeline

Dates are approximate for central and northern states.

November 1: Seeking phase of the rut is in full swing. Some bucks begin to expand their range, wandering out of their home core areas to take the estrous temperature of does within 1000 acres or so. Other big boys roam closer to home, especially in broken farmland where feed and cover are prime. If two dominant deer cross paths, a hair-raising stare down or a heavyweight fight might break out. Watch for a buck "lip curling," or sniffing a doe's urine to check her state of estrus. Bucks keep blazing rubs and pawing scrapes.

November 4: The seeking phase launches into the chasing phase of the rut. Bucks young and old dash at most every doe they see. If a doe smells right, she'll attract several boys, including quite possibly one or two shooters. During the next 2 or 3 weeks, mature bucks may lose 20 to 25 percent of their body weight as they dog and breed does.

November 7: The rut phases merge and it's wild in the woods! You might spot a buck trolling for a doe … or chasing one … or breeding the first gal that pops into estrus. Some bucks rub and scrape haphazardly to vent sexual energy, but the serious sign-posting winds down.

November 10: Give or take a few days, most mature does enter their first estrous cycle. The peak-breeding phase should last roughly 2 weeks in regions where the buck to doe ratio is fairly balanced. Some days you'll spot bucks trolling for does or chasing them. Other days you won't see squat, because the big boys are holed up in thickets, tending and breeding the gals for 1 to 3 days. Studies have shown that bucks impregnate 80 percent or more of the mature does during this time.

November 24: The rut wanes in most areas. Some old, surviving bucks go underground for a few days, resting and licking their wounds. Other big boys go back to checking old scrapes, looking to hook up with a last hot doe.

November 30: The post-rut begins. Some big deer keep cruising and checking scrapes into the first week of December. Does and bucks congregate both in the morning and evening near the best late-season food sources—leftover mast, soybeans, corn, browse, forbs. Rut-thin deer feed like pigs to bulk back up before the cold, snowy winter.

Rut Tips:

➤ Backpack a climber anytime you can. You can move in on a doe trail or scrape line, run your stand up a straight tree and hunt a buck where he's working in a matter of minutes.

➤ Crisp November mornings are best for hunting a ridge or draw back in the timber. Hang tough. A rut-dazed buck might wander by anytime up until 11:00 a.m. If the moon is full, look for increased buck movement from noon till 2:00 p.m.

➤ If you hunt a spot two days without spotting many deer, don't waste more time there. The does have moved, probably to better feed, and the bucks have too. Stay

Move around with a climbing stand and try to get the quick drop on bucks.

mobile, glass for bucks and scout for fresh sign. You might have to move two or three times to score.

➤ Carry a grunt call and horns every day in November. If a buck cruises out of range, grunt or rattle at him. Most of the time he'll at least stop, and he might turn your way.

➤ When gun season opens, monitor where people park their trucks and hike into the woods. Look for a funnel other folks overlook. It might be a mile deep in the woods, or 200 yards off a back road.

➤ Access a ridge or funnel stand from downwind and through "dead woods" every day. Try to get in and out without jumping one deer.

➤ Pack in lunch, water and a pee bottle so you can hunt comfortably for most of, if not all of, the day during peak week.

➤ Lay a doe-in-heat trail into your morning stands. It can actually work better in late November or early December than in the pre-rut because fewer does mist the woods with estrous scent. A cruiser buck crazy for a last doe might cut your trail and zoom in for a look.

➤ If the pressure is not too heavy, keep cracking the horns during Thanksgiving week. In a recent Texas study, biologists rattled in more 3½- to 5½-year-old bucks during the post-rut than they did in the pre-rut or peak.

➤ "If gun hunters overtake all your best spots, scout for an out-of-the-way funnel or pocket of thick brush," says Knight. "There's a good chance your competition will drive some does and bucks in there."

➤ Say you find 30 big scrapes on a ridge one November. Well, if the builder of those scrapes survives the hunting season and the winter and the next summer, he'll likely return to scrape on that same ridge next fall. If you or someone else kills the buck, another male or males should move onto the ridge and rub and paw. Many biologists over the years have confirmed that whitetails are very habitual creatures. Keep hunting heavy rub/scrape pockets year after year.

Studies show that during the rut, either doe or tarsal scent lures bucks with equal effectiveness.

Chapter 7

Today's Late, Great Bowhunting

PITY YOU, for you carry a weighty burden. All your buddies punched their tags weeks or months ago, but you've yet to get your buck. Well, let's see, you've got a couple of options. You can pack it in and whine *I'll get 'em next year.* Or you can bundle up and keep on hunting till the bitter end. I say suck it up and hang tough, for you just might pull a fast one on your buds. There is growing evidence that the post-rut is one of the best times to kill a belly-sagging, gnarly-racked whitetail, an old titan that will make other hunters gawk with envy and wish they hadn't been so release happy earlier in the season. To wit:

"My brother Terry and I hunt and film across the Midwest most every day of the season," says Mark Drury of St. Louis, Missouri. "These days we're seeing more

Your chances of scoring on a big deer are better than you think in December. "You need to plant quality feed on your property, and the colder the weather the better," says Mark Drury.

big deer moving in December than we see in October and even during the November rut. I'm talking about bucks 4½ to 5½ years and older. Thick-chested brutes with racks that score 140 to 150 inches and up."

There is growing scientific support for hunting the post-rut as well. In the late 1990s, a University of Georgia study unearthed a secondary but notable scrape-checking phase that runs from late November through December 9 in central and northern states. It's a time when bucks 2½ years of age and older are really on the move. Also, noted Texas biologist Mick Hellickson recently conducted a study to see how and when deer respond best to rattling. Of the 29 bucks that loped in to the researcher's post-rut rattling sequences, 10 of the animals were 5½ years plus, and another 10 were 3½ or 4½. According to those studies, if you want to kill a monster at a scrape or rattle one in, December is a hot time to do it.

Buck Behavior

As more and more hunters and biologists in central and northern states key on the late season, three theories are emerging as to what triggers the movement of mature bucks then. First, while the peak rut peters out in mid-to-late November in most areas, many old bucks still prowl for weeks for the last estrous does. The boys seem to know that the breeding season won't come around for another year, so they go looking for some last fun into early December.

"We call those big deer 'cruisers,' and we're definitely seeing more and more of them on their feet in the early stages of the post-rut," notes Drury.

Come mid-December, bucks turn their attention from mating to survival. Scraping, chasing and breeding does during the rut, big deer burn up a lot of fuel. Perhaps 40 to 50 pounds lighter than they were back in October and staring down the barrel of a long, tough winter, the animals go back to the filling station and hit whatever high-energy food sources they can find—soybeans, corn, old mast, brassica plants and the like.

Says Drury, "Dr. Grant Woods, the famous deer biologist, once told me, 'Mark, it's pretty simple. Whitetails are slaves to their stomachs, and it's never more obvious than when they're moving to and from feed in December.' The more brother Terry and I hunt the late season, the more we know that Grant is right."

Also, while the last several winters have been seasonal in some regions, much of the U.S. has been in an extended warm, dry pattern for years. In many places, the first serious cold and snow—two proven triggers that make big deer move—haven't hit until early or mid-December. Therefore, warm weather in November has suppressed the rut in places.

Late in the season, Drury shoots most of his bucks in and around fields of corn or soybeans.

"Sooner or later in December you're going to get threatening conditions, with snow and high temperatures in the teens and 20s," points out Drury. "Now your chances of spotting a monster on his feet and moving are pretty darn good. But let me add this. If the mercury shoots back up into the 40s, 50s or even the 60s again, the hunting is definitely going to go back downhill."

Expectations

If we're giving you the impression that you can walk out into a cold, snowy place and see big racks coming out the woodwork, you can *if* you're lucky enough to hunt under ideal conditions. One December, I was a guest at Drury's Iowa farm, a place that my friend has intensively managed for years. The sprawling fields and smaller plots of soybeans, corn, oats and Biologic are interspersed with strips of timber and pockets of security and thermal cover. It is whitetail nirvana and to cap it off, the hunting pressure is tightly controlled.

Most every evening of the hunt I saw 10, 20 or more does rolling out to the feed. Every day I encountered at least one good buck, including a 160-inch 9-pointer that

Keep scouting and hunting hard in the post-rut; you never know when or where you'll spot a buck dogging one of the last hot does. Lucas Strommen photo.

broke my heart and got away. On the fifth evening of the trip, I killed a fine, thick-bodied 8-pointer.

That was awesome. But out in the real world where I normally hunt—and where you probably hunt too—it's not nearly that easy. Come December on all public areas and most private farms, woodlands, and leases, there's been pressure and a lot of it—people stomping around, riding ATVs, shooting rifles or shotguns, making drives, etc. Some big bucks have been removed from the gene pool by either broadheads or bullets. The survivors are skittish and nocturnal as vampires. You've hunted all day in December without seeing a buck and maybe only a few does right?

Well, keep the faith and keep hunting. Some big deer still roam your woods, and a last hot doe or the powerful draw of feed will get them on their hooves and stirring. Try to hunt a cold, calm day in the middle of the week, when few, if any, other people are in the woods. The day before, or especially the two days after, a snow can be a magical time to be out there.

"I'll take 2 inches of snow, but I prefer 5 or 6 inches," says Drury. "A fairly deep snow covers all the leftover acorns and other mast and foodstuffs in the woods. That causes deer to pour out into fields. If you thought

ahead and planted some plots specifically for post-rut hunting, you'll be in great shape."

Scrape Redux

From Thanksgiving through the first week of December, some old bucks go back and check scrapes they pawed in late October and early November. It makes sense if you think about it. Near those scrapes is where the studs hooked up with the first estrous does. That's where they might run across a last gal hot to trot.

You should go back too. Scout major scrapes and scrape lines you located a month ago, working a key ingredient—cover—into your strategy. Any good buck in his right mind that survived a hail of arrows and bullets earlier in the season will check scrapes in the thickest pockets he can find.

Set up downwind of "cover scrapes" with fresh sign. "The more major doe trails that cut through an area the better," notes Drury. "Watch for a buck running one of those."

Here's a new piece of science that you really need to know. The Georgia study I alluded to earlier found that while one set of scrapes on a ridge might go stone

cold, multiple bucks and does might tear up scrapes on a ridge or in a bottom only 100 or 200 yards away. So you need to constantly cover lots of ground in search of the hottest scrapes, and then hunt right there. That goes for either the pre-rut or the post-rut.

"If you hunt old scrapes and doe trails correctly, not necessarily sitting smack on top of them but maybe backing off a bit and watching a hogback, draw or linear thicket that leads to the sign, you stand a darn good chance of seeing a cruiser buck in late November or early December," says Drury.

The cruisers should move best at dawn and dusk during a dark moon phase in a central or northern state. The colder the better, and a little snow wouldn't hurt.

On a crisp, still morning back in the timber, try a few last volleys of rattling. "It can still work because some dominant bucks are still cruising for the last hot does," says Drury. "But man, you've got to be cautious. In some areas, other hunters have rattled at bucks since the first of October, so big deer might be leery. We tone it down. In fact, we hardly ever rattle blind during the post-rut. If we make visual contact with a buck upwind, we might tick the horns to get his attention and hopefully pull him our way."

Key on Feed

If you bowhunt farm country in mid-December and possibly into January, focus your efforts around fields of corn, soybeans, wheat and the like. Obviously, the more feed left standing or scattered on the ground the better. "We've found that whitetails prefer a cut field as opposed to a standing one," notes Drury. "When you or a farmer harvests a field, all the residue, be it soybeans or corn, lies on the ground, absorbs moisture, softens up and becomes highly palatable to deer. Also, it is easier for does and bucks to move around and feed in a low, cut field than in standing crops."

Sacrifice a couple of your last hunting days to scout the feed fields. Now mentally, that's tough. You feel like you ought to be out there going like hell and trying to fill your last tag. But two or three days of low-impact glassing can pay off big time.

"In fact, anytime of season you ought to scout and observe deer as much or more than you hunt them," says Drury. "Hanging a tree stand or setting up a ground blind for a 30-yard shot at a giant buck is tough. Sometimes it just seems impossible. It takes hours, days and sometimes weeks of observation before you can find just the right spot."

Drive to an area around 2:00 one afternoon. Hide your truck out of sight and mind of deer. Bundle up, hike to a vantage and start glassing fields and plots 400 to 500 yards below. A procession of does and spindly-

When deer eat up all the grain in one plot, they'll move to the next best food source. Move your stand over there, too.

racked bucks will generally show first, followed by a brute or two at dusk (hopefully).

The second you spot a good buck stop gawking at his rack! Instead, focus on where he popped out of the brush or timber. Visualize a line to his bedding area. And where might that be? Well, in winter many bucks seek shelter on the first east- or south-facing slope off a field, where they curl up tight to the feed and out of the bitter west or northwest wind. An old buck might vary his approach from the woods to a field every afternoon. But if he pops out the same corner or edge two or three days running, perfect. You've patterned him as best you can. Now, go for an ambush.

Obviously, the wind can't blow back toward a trail or bedding cover in the timber, but it can't swirl out into a spot in a field where does will pop out first either. Try to go in and set up on an edge where your scent will blow across and back into "dead woods" where few, if any, deer are apt to approach your stand or blind.

Speaking of stands and blinds, "I do most of my bowhunting out of trees, but I never pass up the opportunity to set up on the ground, especially late in the sea-

Many tracks lead to a south-facing hillside where deer feed and rest out of the wind and in the midday sun.

slip into and out of a field-side post without a single deer seeing you. If just one jumpy old doe eyeballs you and starts stamping and blowing, you probably won't see your buck that night. Heck, you might never see him again. If you can't use a ditch, creek bank, brush or the like to cover your moves, don't risk it. If you bump one doe back in the timber, you'll spook a bunch of deer.

Now many of you hunt private or public woodlands where the nearest corn or bean field is miles away. Your hunting won't be nearly so good late in the season, but still you need to go to the feed, in this case, the "secondary feed." Every woodlot has some.

Scout a ridge, draw or creek bottom where you found big rubs and scrapes back in November. If you find huge tracks in the mud or snow, or big prints mixed in with a bunch of doe tracks, you can figure a good buck is still working the area.

Now poke about for the last scraps of food. Deer paw through leaves or snow to get at wild apples, cherries, Osage orange, acorns, beechnuts, or any other old mast they can find.

Check your maps for a 2- or 3-year-old cutover, burn, or pine plantation in the area. A regenerating thicket provides great thermal cover for skittish bucks, but enough sunlight filters through in spring and summer to grow honeysuckle, greenbrier and other browse. The edges of power or gas lines are also great places to hunt, as the strips hold browse and provide decent cover for bucks.

When you go in to hang a stand or set a blind, get the wind right and access your post smartly. "Skirt bedding areas and, again, try not to spook a single deer on your way in or out," says Drury. "Get on stand early each morning. In the afternoons, stay until well after legal shooting light fades."

Don't overlook the midday hours. Since a big deer feels sort of safe and hidden back in the timber or in a big cutover or thicket, he might get up to stretch and browse at 10:00 a.m., noon or 2:00 p.m. Hang tough on post and you might yet arrow a giant that will turn your buddies green with envy.

son," notes Drury. "Actually, in December you're often better off on the ground than 20 feet up a tree. You'll stay warmer, and if you set up right, you'll have better cover."

When the situation warrants it, build a grass, brush or log blind on a point, hillside or field edge with a good view of a feeding area or a trail or funnel that leads out into crops. Watch the wind and know exactly where your scent will disperse as you set up for a 20- to 30-yard shot.

Since whitetails are stressed and wired now, access to your stand or blind is critical. Your goal should be to

When the countryside freezes over, look for pockets of open water and feed. You'll see deer. Lucas Strommen photo.

Late-Season Tips:

➤ Staying warm begins with staying dry, and staying dry begins with wearing high-performance undergarments. You'll definitely want to check out Underarmour's new Cold Gear for hunters *(www.underarmour.com)*. The mock turtles and leggings are similar to what the NFL players wear, only the hunters' versions come in black, olive or brown. The tight-fitting, two-layer garments wick sweat, break the wind and keep you warmer in subfreezing temperatures than any other undergarments I've ever worn. Plus, they're incredibly thin and lightweight, which allows you to climb into tree stands and draw your bow with ease. Top things off with a Cold Gear mask and you'll be ready to hunt on brutally cold days when big bucks move best.

➤ Cabela's MTP (Maximum Thermal Protection) undergarments also work well. The polyester tops and bottoms not only wick sweat from your skin, but they also have Scent Eliminator technology woven into the fabric.

➤ Both Drury and I like to layer up with Scent Blocker's Evolution Fleece *(www.robinso noutdoors.com)*. The combination of fleece/charcoal-activated lining makes the pullover and pants soft, warm, quiet and scent-free. Pack along a Mossy Oak Gore-Tex shell for rain or snow.

➤ If it's brutally cold and you wear several shirts and jackets, wear an extra-long armguard that compresses the sleeves along the inside of your forearm and up to your bicep. Your bowstring should drop smoothly and freely when you shoot at a mega buck.

➤ Your socks are as important as your boots. Wear thin, perspiration-wicking liners (polypropylene or Thermastat) and wool or synthetic outer socks.

➤ As a rule for leather boots, choose 200 grams of Thinsulate for moderate conditions, 400 to 600 grams when it's cold, and 800 to 1000 grams when it's bitter and snowy. Wear boots lined with Scent-Lok or Supprescent.

➤ Rubber-bottom "pacs" are your best defense against brutally cold temperatures. If you hunt deer in an upper-south state like Virginia, boots with a "warmth rating" of minus 30 or 40

A pasture or power line with edges of browse and thermal cover is a good place to fill your last buck tag.

should be fine. In the frigid, snowy Midwest or Northeast, opt for minus 100 to 135 pacs.

➤ Stuff your pockets with Hot Hands to keep your fingers (especially that release finger!) limber and ready.

➤ On a cold day, look around every 30 minutes or so and make sure no deer are coming. Draw your bow a couple of times to keep your shooting muscles limber and ready for action.

➤ Try a gel scent, which won't freeze up as quickly as a liquid, and which will float the strong stench of a last hot doe or a still-rutting intruder buck for hours.

➤ Early to mid-December is a great time to lay an estrous-doe trail into your stand. Bucks are still cruising hard for the last hot does, but there are relatively few receptive gals now. A buck might cut your scent trail and nose it right to your stand.

➤ Whenever possible, saw out a spot for a lock-on stand in a cedar or pine tree. The evergreen will break the wind, provide you with excellent cover and add natural cover scent to your setup.

➤ You cut big tracks in the snow—buck or old doe? A mature buck's stride is noticeably longer than a doe's, and his fat, splayed prints are often linked with "drag lines."

Chapter 8

The Buck Shooter's Plan

Chuck Jones's Number One shooting rule: Don't fire at a whole deer, but rather focus on a tiny patch of hide behind a buck's shoulder and put your arrow right there.

THE SECOND YOU SPOT AN OLD, hip-swaying, gnarly-racked buck mincing toward your tree stand, you need to stand up, pluck your bow off a hook, shift your feet and turn your body toward the deer, raise your bow, draw, fine-tune a sight pin on a patch of hair on his side, wait until the critter is inside 30 yards and turned just right, and *finally* cut loose an arrow. If I counted correctly, you have to make at least eight critical moves with your hands shaking and your heart tripping like a jackhammer in your chest. Use this 9-step plan to pull it all together and lance bucks through the boiler room.

73

This is a close—but tough—shot because all you can see is a buck's spine. Set up where deer will angle in 10 to 25 yards out and expose their lung vitals.

1 **Set up smartly.** Play smart long before you lay eyes on a big deer. Do you normally hang a tree stand 16 to 18 feet high? Well, move it on up to 20 or 22 or even higher. "I like to hunt extremely high," says Chuck Jones of Cadiz, Kentucky. "Extra elevation gives you more and better visibility, puts your wind way above the deer and lets you get away with some movement as a buck approaches."

In addition to a fear of heights, many hunters don't like the severe shooting angle down to a deer when you hunt in a skyscraper stand. But Jones has learned to deal with that by shooting at a lot of 3-D targets from high towers and stands. "It's really no big deal if you practice and get used to the sight picture of a deer's side and vitals. I want be way up a tree so a buck can't pick me off."

After scouting out a spot with fresh rubs,

scrapes or feed, don't just stick a stand on a tree, but rather position it so you'll never have to make a big, fancy move as a deer approaches. "I always try face my stand into the wind and in the direction I think a buck will come from," notes Jones. "That way I don't have to move much at all when I see him."

Tweak your setup even more. If you shoot right-handed, position a perch so your left shoulder points toward the down-and-to-the-left lane where you hope to see and shoot a deer (vice versa for southpaws). If a buck shows up in that shooting hole or close to it, your body and feet will be in good starting position for a shot, and you'll be able to move and draw with little movement.

The Kentucky pro loves to hunt thick areas for old bucks, but he gets nervous when he has to hang a stand in a spot where he can see only

50 yards or so. "In a tight setup, the first time you see a big deer he might be right on top of you, in bow range and maybe even standing in your best shooting lane. You might not have the time you need to make good moves and decisions and get off a lethal shot. You might get excited and try to draw and shoot quickly. A buck is likely to look up and bust you or, worse, you might touch off a poor shot and miss or wound him."

For those reasons, Jones always tries to set a stand extremely high or on an edge of thick cover where he can see deer coming for at least 100 yards. He can watch and read a buck for a few min-

Don't let a limb catch your bow or deflect an arrow. Trim a clean spot for your stand and three or four good shooting lanes.

utes and make the right moves, all the while calming his nerves as he sets up the shot.

2 Get Ready. Climb into a tree stand and organize your gear. If you're right-handed, set your bow on a hook or limb within inches of your left hand. Try to hang it a couple feet out in front of you, where you can reach out and grab it with virtually no movement the instant you spot a buck. Also, hang your binoculars, range finder, rattling horns and the like on hooks within easy reach. In short, get organized *before* a buck shows up. You'll move less, make less noise and overall be more efficient and ready to go if and when the moment of truth arrives.

3 Stand or Sit? Once in a blue moon, a buck will stroll in and stop in the optimum spot, 15 to 20 yards down and to the left of your perch. Assuming you're a right-hander, you could remain seated, hold your bow off to the left or out front between your knees, draw and fire an arrow with virtually no movement.

If you shoot right-handed, hang a stand where a buck will come in out front or down to your left.

The Buck Shooter's Plan

Concentrate and scan the woods for a flash of hide or antler. The farther out you pick up a buck, the longer you have to set up the shot.

"It's important to learn to sit and shoot at deer so you can take advantage of those few perfect situations," says Jones, who practices sitting down and generally kills at least one good buck that way each fall.

The other nine out of 10 times whitetails are generally not so obliging. Regardless of how well you scout, play the wind and tweak a stand on a tree, you never really know where a buck will show up within 30 yards one day. He might come in out front, off to the right, or even from behind. A deer might start in from the coveted left, only to circle out front or to the extreme right, where it is tough to impossible for a right-hander to draw and shoot while sitting down.

I believe you're best off standing on a platform, at least when it comes time to shoot at a deer. You can shift your feet and turn your body to shoot a buck anywhere in the 180-degree arc out front of your perch, or even 90 degrees to the left and behind it (again, for the right-handed shooter). Besides, most hunters practice standing up, and hence they feel most comfortable and confident drawing and shooting that way.

I know hunters who stand all the time to take the one major move out of the deer-shooting equation. The guys have conditioned themselves to stand on a platform for hours. They lean back against a tree and put their weight on one foot, and then awhile later, shift their weight to the other foot. They go back and forth like that all morning or afternoon.

If you can hack it, do it. If you can't, don't sweat it. There's nothing wrong with sitting for long spells in a perch. In fact, there are benefits. You are more comfortable and thus more likely to stay still, and your body doesn't get fatigued. Just don't get too comfortable. Stay on the edge of your seat and be ready to stand up quickly when a big deer rolls onto the scene.

4 Look and Listen. Standing or sitting, it's tough to stay on red-alert for hours, especially when it's cold or rainy and you haven't seen a buck for a while. But you gotta stay sharp. The minute you drop your guard and start daydreaming, presto! a monster will pop up within 50 yards or so of your stand. You never want that.

"As I said earlier, when a big deer surprises you, you tend to get rattled, make a fast, foolish move and spook him," says Jones. "So you always need to concentrate. Scan the woods and try to pick up the flash of antlers or hide as far out you as can. You'll have time to calm your nerves, stand up if you have to, shift your body into position and plan your draw and shot."

I've got to tell you a little story. I once hunted out in the big-buck woods of the Midwest for five long days and never saw a shooter. Six hours into the sixth day, I heard a stick crack, then one snort. I raised my PSE, grunted in the nick of time, stopped the 150-inch bruiser that trotted below my stand and ran an aluminum arrow through his heart. The encounter took all of 20 seconds! No matter how vigilant you are, things can happen that fast, so look and *listen* hard. One good thing about a quickie hunt is that you don't have time to get the buck fever. Just react and kill a deer if and when you can.

5 Read A Buck. One day you glimpse a fine animal 120 yards out, angling toward your stand, taking his sweet time, his rack big and brassy in the sun. Do not, I repeat, do not take your eyes off the deer for even a second. If you look over to grab your bow or pick up your binocular, you might look back up and he'll be

Notice the ladder stand and block target in the background. The more you draw and shoot your bow from a backyard stand, the better the deer shot you'll be. Lucas Strommen photo.

gone—down in a ditch, behind a hump, in a thicket, whatever. It might take you a couple of frantic minutes to pick him up again. Heck, you might never see him again.

Jones recommends a sort of double vision. "Watch a buck with one eye and with your other eye look 20 to 40 yards ahead of him for trails, holes and open lanes in the cover. Take a quick read of the terrain and brush, and try to predict where and how he'll approach your stand."

It's important to read a buck's body language early on in an encounter. "Things are good when a big deer is calm and strolls along with his head down and his hindquarters swaying," notes the Kentucky pro. "He doesn't know you're in the world. But anytime a buck looks tense and nervous, say he constantly stops and starts and throws up his head and looks all around, you've got to be extra careful. Man, he'll bust you in a second if you make a wrong move."

6 Move It. Most of the time an encounter works out so that a buck walks into a thicket … dips into a ditch or draw … moves behind the lip of a ridge … sticks his head behind a tree … or turns to look over his back trail at another deer. Whatever the case, move when his eyes are covered. Hug the tree, stand up, grab your bow and turn your body toward the deer. "Make one smooth, quick and confident move," notes Jones. "Don't be tentative."

Things get trickier when several deer approach your stand, perhaps moving toward a feeding area or back to bed one morning. With all those laser eyes out there, you've got to be super careful.

Often there will be a sentry in the bunch, quite likely an alpha doe. "If you move at the wrong time or do something foolish, an old doe will pick you off and often start head-bobbing, stomping and blowing," says Jones. "She'll alert any bucks in the area that something is wrong. Keep your eye on an old gal and move only

The Buck Shooter's Plan

If you're tough enough to stand for hours, great. You'll be still, hidden and super-ready when a buck shows up.

when she's hidden by a tree or brush, or looking away or back at other deer."

Watch as many deer as you can, and when the coast appears mostly clear, take a chance, lean back into the tree and push your body up slowly. Stay planted against the bark, at least for the time being. "The tighter you stay to a tree, the more movement you can get away with because the trunk, branches and leaves offer some cover," notes Jones.

7 Fancy Footwork. At this point in an encounter, your footwork is all-important. I'll assume you're familiar with the basic mechanics of hitting a baseball. Position your feet on a stand's platform like a right-handed batter with a slightly open stance. You're in perfect shooting position, body pointed left and toward an incoming buck. Pan with the deer as he walks into the front-left arc. Fine-tune your position and draw and shoot when you can.

On the flip side, a buck that sneaks in to the right of a right-handed archer is big trouble. That 90-degree arc from directly right of your stand to directly behind it is "no man's land."

Draw when a buck steps behind a tree or turns his head to look back at other deer.

When you hear hoof beats in this area, freeze. Cut your eyes right and try to pick up the deer as quickly as possible. If you see him step into a ditch or thicket or move behind a little slope, grab your bow and stand up. Turn slightly right on the platform to get a better view of the buck, "but don't try to contort all the way around and face him," notes Jones. "If you move and twist too much, he'll probably bust you. You might get all tied up in your harness, and you won't have a good shot anyway."

Stay cool and collected and watch the buck. He might walk in from the right-rear angle, cruise beneath your perch and offer a broadside or quartering-away shot out front of your stand. He might pull a fast one and sneak in behind your perch, going from right to left. "Things get tricky with the wind and all, but you're still in pretty good shape if you keep your wits," says the pro. Let the buck go and hope he doesn't smell you. Hold your bow close to your body

and turn slowly back to the left. Your tree will be squarely between you and the buck, and it will help cover your moves.

Here again, your footwork is critical. As you shift your body left, position your boots on the platform like a left-handed batter with an open stance. You're ready to draw and shoot if the buck reappears in a shooting lane to the left and behind your stand.

8 Draw Time. When a buck walks or trots on a line for your stand and an open shooting lane within 30 yards, draw your bow as soon as you can, perhaps when he steps behind a tree 40 to 50 yards out. That will give you enough time—but not too much time—to calm your nerves, settle your bow, pick the right pin and kill the deer when he walks past in a few seconds.

If a buck is chasing a doe, draw sooner yet, while he's still a good ways out there. Don't let him gallop past before you can touch off a shot! I wouldn't worry too much about waiting for a rut-dazed buck to look away or go behind a tree. He's locked in on his gal and thinking wicked thoughts. Most of the time, you can pull your bow while he's in the wide open, and he'll never know you're in the world. "Grunt or whistle to stop the buck the second he rolls into a shooting hole, but be sure to come to full draw before you do," adds Jones.

Things are different when a buck takes his sweet time mincing toward your stand, meandering and stopping here and there to browse or rub his eyes and pre-orbital scent on dangling branches. Resist the urge to draw too early. You sure don't want to come to full pull about the time he hangs up 50 or 60 yards out. If he tarries, you'll quiver and shake until you can't hold the poundage any longer. If you have to let down and then draw again, you're almost sure to get busted.

In this scenario, let a deer stroll smack into shooting range, and then take your chances and draw. If cover is sparse, let the deer walk a few yards past your stand so that he is looking and quartering away. "That is always your best shot," says Jones.

I rarely drop the bowstring until a whitetail is inside 30 yards. A 20- or even a 10-yard broadside or quartering-away shot is better yet.

9 Close the Deal. In my opinion you shouldn't drop the bowstring until a buck is inside 40 yards—30 yards is better—and inside 25 yards is always best. Many guys talk a good game about shooting deer out to 40 and 50 yards and even beyond. But as the range extends, so do most hunters' arrow groups. Further, the effects of a whitetail hearing the twang of a bowstring and then "jumping" that sound are magnified at 35 yards and beyond. If a buck is way out there and drops and whirls like 90 percent of them seem to do, you're likely to miss or, worse, make a wounding shot. Bottom line: The closer the buck the better.

Always shoot for quick, clean, double-lung kills. That means flying an arrow only when a buck is broadside, quartering away or quartering *slightly* to. That's it! Anybody who intentionally shoots for the neck or the femoral artery in a buck's ham should have his archery license revoked. If a deer, no matter the size of its rack, never turns and presents a clear lane to both lungs, hold your fire. It is the right thing to do.

On a broadside animal, "aim at the point of the shoulder, or in the crease just behind the front leg," says Jones. I'll add to hone in on a tiny patch of hide a third of the way up the deer's body. If he stands still at the shot, you might clip the top of the heart as well as the lungs. If he ducks at the sound of your bow going off, you should center punch both lungs.

On a quartering-away shot remember to move your sight pin back on the ribs so you won't shoot a buck too far forward in the bony, meaty shoulder. The more severe the going-away angle, the farther back on the ribs you need to aim to punch an arrow forward into the lungs.

Now you're ready. "Pull an arrow when you can, let it go in one smooth motion and remember to follow through," says Jones. "Watch the fletching disappear into a big deer's lungs. There's no better feeling."

Shooting Tips:

A sitting shot at a buck is rare but great. Draw and fire with little movement.

➤ During your backyard practice sessions in the summer, condition your mind and eye to stay on target. Bore your eye through a peep sight and watch every arrow disappear into the lungs of a 3-D target. You can sometimes will an arrow to hit where you aim if you concentrate, focus on a spot and follow through.

➤ The best practice is to simulate a hunt. If you typically hunt 18 to 22 feet up a tree, hang a stand 18 to 22 feet high in your backyard,

climb up and shoot a ton of arrows at 3-D targets and blocks over the summer. Set your foam deer at various yardages and at broadside and quartering angles.

➤ Once deer season opens, shoot *one* arrow tipped with a broadhead each day. You're lucky if you get one shot at a good buck each fall. The physical and especially the mental benefits of your everyday one-shot practice will help you make that one shot count in the woods. Of course, it never hurts to shoot more on the weekends to keep your shooting eye sharp and your muscles toned.

➤ After climbing into a tree stand and roping up your bow, check for junk in and around the cables, split limbs and especially the cams. Dirt, weeds or twigs can get jammed into your bow and cause all sorts of problems when you try to draw and shoot.

➤ The second you determine a buck is a shooter, take your eyes off that gorgeous 8- or 10-point rack and never look at it again. This is especially important if the deer is a giant that will score 150 or 160 or more. The longer you stare and marvel at a huge mass of bone, the more apt you are to get nervous or succumb to the buck fever. Besides, as a deer gets close, you need to hone in not on antlers but on the tiny patch of hide you'll shoot at. After making a good killing shot, you can hold and study those awesome antlers all you want.

➤ On the rare occasion when you have to shoot at a walking deer, remember to lead him slightly. "That's hard to do, but you have to make yourself," says Jones. "I recently shot at a buck walking toward a decoy. I aimed on the point of his shoulder, but I didn't take into account how fast he was walking. The arrow hit far back in lungs and liver. I got lucky and killed the deer, but I should have lead him a lot more."

Chapter 9

Find Your Buck

Brad Farris has trailed and recovered hundreds of bowshot whitetails. "If you don't see a buck fall, wait an hour or more before trailing, even if you think you made a perfect shot," he says.

YOUR GOAL IS TO ZIP AN ARROW and a broadhead through both lungs of a buck, possibly piercing the heart as well if your shot was low and extra true. But let's not duck reality. Upon hearing the *swish* of even the quietest bowstring, many whitetails come unglued and come out of their skin. For years, hunters have called it "jumping the string" but that is a misnomer. Starting today, we ought to call it the "dip and whirl." When an old doe or buck reacts to a bowshot, it drops its chest almost flat to the ground and whirls back and away one way or another. You can't see it with the naked eye because they do it so fast, but slow-mo a video of an animal ducking an arrow and you'll be flat-out amazed.

Also, a perfectly aimed arrow might clip a tree limb and veer a few inches or a foot offline. With your knees

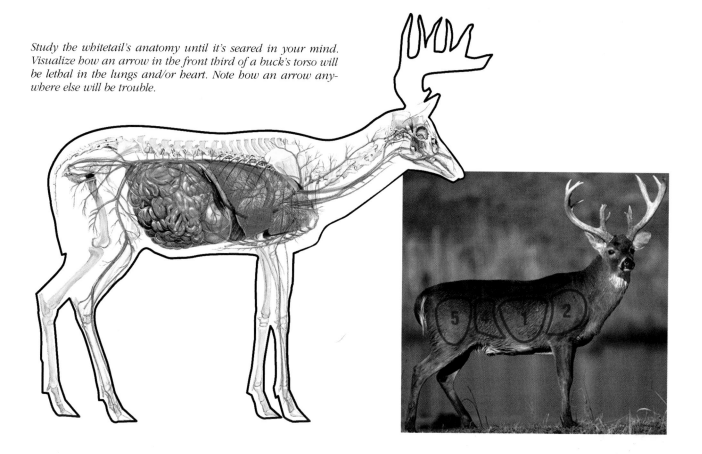

Study the whitetail's anatomy until it's seared in your mind. Visualize how an arrow in the front third of a buck's torso will be lethal in the lungs and/or heart. Note how an arrow anywhere else will be trouble.

shaking and your heart tripping like a jackhammer as you squint through a peep at a giant rack, you might get rattled and yank a release's trigger instead of pressing it. You might choose your 30-yard pin for a 22-yard shot. Get my drift? All sorts of things can cause a gimme bowshot to go amiss.

Sail an arrow cleanly over or under a deer and that's okay. It's frustrating, but at least the animal will live to see another day. But when you hit a doe or buck in any of the five anatomical zones I've outlined here, it's your duty to work long and hard until you find it. To help in your recovery efforts, I asked Brad Farris of Primos Hunting Calls for some expert advice. For several years, Farris was head guide at Tara Wildlife's Willow Point lodge, one of Mississippi's top archery-only operations. Through his work there and with the Primos video crew, the guy has trailed and found literally hundreds of bowshot deer.

Zone 1: Bull's Eye!

Hit: Perfect! Your broadhead and arrow can't help but cut and collapse major organs. Depending on whether a buck stands broadside or quarters slightly away, and depending upon precisely where the shaft hits and penetrates inside this zone, you'll get both lungs and maybe the heart, or at least one lung and maybe the heart.

Reaction: "A deer might kick his hind legs way up, take off like a shot and run until it dies," says Farris. "Or he might run hard for a ways, stop and fall over dead." Either way, that is what you want!

Clues: Look for your arrow at the point of impact. If the shaft doesn't hit too much rib or shoulder bone, it will often zip clean through a broadside animal and stick in the ground on the other side. "Usually the arrow will be covered from broadhead to nock with bright blood with some bubbles," notes Farris. "Cut hair on the ground will be brown or gray."

If an arrow catches shoulder bone at the very front tip of this zone, it probably won't penetrate fully. An aluminum shaft might break off as the animal bolts. You might find the top part of the arrow anywhere from the point of impact to 20 or 50 yards down the trail where the deer fled. Regarding that trail, "blood will be sprayed or blown out along the way," adds Farris.

Trail pointers: Double-lung an animal and it won't live more than 10 seconds or so. It will be dead on its hooves and will fall within 100 yards. Walk out, check your arrow, pick up the spectacular blood trail

An arrow that blew through both lungs of a buck is usually covered with blood from broadhead to nock. You'll find that deer within 100 yards.

Pink to red blood with bubbles indicates an arrow clipped at least one lung and hopefully both of them.

and go get your buck. "But if you didn't see him fall from your tree stand or blind, wait an hour or so before trailing just to be on the safe side."

Recently in Illinois, Farris drilled a buck perfectly. Or so he and his cameraman thought as they reviewed the tape of the hunt from their tree stands. "The arrow passed through the deer, but when I picked it up, it just didn't look right," he says. "It wasn't covered from end to end with blood." He thought that was strange, and after following the red trail for 100 yards without finding the buck, he knew something was wrong. "I backed out right then and there."

When the Mississippi pro came back the next morning, he found the buck dead in a bed 150 yards from where he had stopped the previous evening. A quick, in-the-field autopsy confirmed that the arrow had clipped only one lung and missed the liver entirely. There is a lesson here. "If you think you double-lunged a buck but don't find him within 100 yards, that tells you your arrow got only one lung," says Farris. "Don't push that deer. Let him lie down up ahead and die. He shouldn't be too far, maybe within another 200 yards." The pro recommends you wait at least 4 hours before trailing, or if on an afternoon hunt, leave the animal overnight.

Go slow, get down on your hands and knees and look hard for specks of blood.

Zone 2: Too Much Shoulder

Hit: I believe that many people are so afraid of paunch-shooting a deer that they unwittingly aim a little too far forward at times. Try to sneak an arrow too tight behind a buck's front leg, and it is easy to plant it a few inches too far forward into the bony, meaty shoulder. This is especially true when an animal is quartering away. To avoid this poor hit, move your aiming point back a few inches and shoot for the biggest part of the lungs. They extend a third of the way back on a whitetail.

If you can't find your arrow at the point of impact, look for a snapped part of it 50 to 100 yards down a trail where a buck ran.

Sometimes an arrowed buck will run to a familiar trail and flee along it. Check there for blood.

hair on the broadhead and a little blood on the bottom of the arrow); or an aluminum arrow might snap off. Look for the top of the shaft within 50 to 100 yards of where the deer ran. There won't be a lot of blood to begin with, and it will probably peter out rather quickly. Every once in a blue moon, you'll get lucky. The arrow will zip just under the heavy scapula and clip the front tip of the lungs.

"Hit a deer low in the brisket, and you'll usually find a lot of bright blood on the ground," notes Farris. "If you find your arrow, it might have brown or white hair on it, some meat and fat, but surprisingly not much blood on it."

Reaction: "A buck hit in the shoulder or brisket will generally run off low in the front end and off to one side," notes Farris. "He'll appear ready to stumble any minute the first 50 to 75 yards, but he'll usually keep going."

Clues: Listen for a loud *th-waack*, although the sound of your arrow hitting heavy shoulder bone is not something you want to hear. I've seen arrows hit squarely on a deer's big, flat shoulder blade and bounce straight back after the animal ran a few yards! But more often, a high-shoulder hit results in a "hanger," with the arrow penetrating a few inches and then flopping as the deer runs off. Farris notes that an aluminum or carbon arrow might then fall out (you'll find meat and brown

Trail pointers: Farris notes that if you hit a deer low in the side of the chest, you might find lots of blood the first 200 to 300 yards, but then it will usually dry up. "Wait 30 to 60 minutes before looking. It's hard to give a percentage of recovery on this very marginal shot." The Mississippi pro points out that if you got lucky and cut major veins or an artery, you might find a buck stone dead. "But I've seen a lot of deer survive these hits."

Wait a while before looking for a whitetail shot high in the shoulder. If you got super-lucky and the shaft penetrated deeply enough to find the front tip of a lung(s), a buck will die, though he might go a good ways. But if the arrow went in a few inches and backed out or broke off, you are not going to find him. The good news is that the deer should live and be fine.

Blood and cut hair at the point of impact are your first and primary points of reference. Mark the spot with orange tape and come back to it if you lose the blood trail.

Zone 3: No Man's Land

Hit: Many people aim too high at deer, especially when shooting down from a tree stand. I've given this a lot of thought, and I believe it's because at 20 feet up, we tend to see a buck as farther away than he really is, no matter how much we've used our range finder. Anyhow, if you shoot for the upper half of a buck's lungs and pull the shot just inches high, your arrow might hit in the elongated oval I call "no man's land." Sometimes this works out and you hit the spine or the aorta that runs down a deer's back. But more often, you'll miss those vitals and strike only soft tissue in the upper back.

Remember what we said earlier about many whitetails dipping and whirling at the sound of your bow going off. If a buck drops a few inches or a foot or more, your arrow will obviously strike high. Remember also what we said in the previous chapter on shooting. To avoid a highly marginal hit in this zone, aim for the lower third of a buck's vitals. If he drops at the shot,

your arrow should still take him in the middle or top of the lungs. If he stands still as some calm deer do, you make a perfect heart/low lung shot.

Reaction: If the arrow hits low enough to catch one or more of the spinal processes that extend up from a deer's vertebrae, an animal will go straight down or stagger down. On rare occasions, an animal will thrash, recover and lunge off. Think fast and put another arrow into the deer if you can.

On the other hand, when an arrow misses the spine and the main artery that runs down the back, "I have seen deer simply jump from the noise of the shot, look around and walk or run off, depending on how badly they were spooked," adds Farris.

Clues: Your buck might lay right there before your eyes if you got lucky and spined him. If he fled, check the point of impact for long, dark-brown back hair. There will be plenty of bright blood if your arrow severed the aorta. But much of the time, you'll find your

Find Your Buck

arrow smeared with fat and flesh but little blood. "It missed the spine and artery and simply went through the soft back tissue," notes Farris.

Trail pointers: A deer with a severed aortic artery will not go far, maybe 60 to 75 yards, and there will be a good blood spray to follow. Farris recommends you wait a half-hour or so before trailing just to be on the safe side. "Recovery will be 100 percent on spine and artery hits, though you got lucky," he says. "You should never aim high for those spots."

When an arrow zips through flesh only on a buck's back, you'll generally find little blood at the point of impact and on down the trail. It makes no difference how long you wait before following—you won't find him! The good news is that the deer will live to see another season and grow a bigger rack. Farris told me that down at Tara, he used to see a lot of bucks running around at full speed with healed wounds on their upper backs.

Zone 4: A Little Too Far Back

Hit: Try as you might not to do it, you will hit some deer too far back if you archery hunt very much. If your arrow lands in the very front of this zone, you can sigh a little bit of relief because it might clip the back of the lungs and probably the liver. There's no nice or easy way to say this, but a hit back in the rear two-thirds of this area will get only paunch or guts.

Reaction: A deer may hump up as if it were kicked in the stomach when the arrow strikes. But often, it will simply drop its tail and run like the wind, giving little or no indication of a hit. "Typically a buck runs 50 to 75 yards and stops," notes Farris. "Sometimes he'll stand humped up. Then he will either lie down or walk off slowly." Rarely will a gut-shot deer go more than 200 to 250 yards before it beds down for the first time.

Clues: If your arrow hit far enough forward to pierce the liver, you'll find a little or a lot of dark blood on the shaft and ground, along with brown hair. An arrow that passes through a paunch is generally covered with slimy green matter, brown and white belly hair and traces of watery blood. You'll often find stomach or intestinal contents and fragments strewn about the hit area and along the path the deer fled.

Trail pointers: A deer shot through the liver won't go far, and it will lie down and die pretty quickly. Wait an hour, follow a trail of dark-red blood and you should have little trouble finding your game. On the

other hand, "don't trail a deer hit in the guts for at least 8 to 10 hours," says Farris. "I recommend waiting at least 12 hours, or overnight if it's cool, to let the deer bed down a few times and die. You've got a good chance of recovering that animal if you don't pressure it at all."

Zone 5: Way Too Far Back

Hit: Anybody who aims at a whitetail's hindquarter should have his archery license revoked, but hits do occur way back there on occasion. Your arrow might clip a branch and veer back into a ham. Or a deer might whirl frantically at the sound of the shot and throw his butt into the flight of your arrow as he tries to flee. A big Montana 10-pointer did that to me (Hanback) not long ago. I found him, and I'll tell you how in the following sections.

Reaction: "A deer will run off fast with his hindquarters low and usually falling off to one side," notes Farris. If the arrow strikes smack in the hip joint, a buck might go down, but he'll generally thrash and stagger back up. Again, get another arrow in him if you can.

Clues: Often an arrow will stick in the hindquarter and break as a deer churns frantically away. Look for meat, tissue and long, dark hair on the shaft and on the ground. The ham is one of the most richly blooded anatomical parts of a deer. It is almost impossible for an arrow and a broadhead not to cause major damage to one or more large blood vessels, even if the femoral artery (about the size of your little finger) that runs down the hip is missed. If you find lots of blood sprayed everywhere at the point of impact and along the escape trail, figure a ham and hope for a lethal femoral hit. That Montana buck I told you about bled more than any deer I have shot over the past 25 years. It looked like somebody had poured thin red paint out of buckets along the trail.

Trail pointers: "If your arrow severs the femoral artery, a deer should go no more than 60 to 80 yards and die on his feet in seconds," says Farris. "But if you do not see him fall, I would wait a few hours before looking just to be safe." That advice is great 95 percent of the time, but I need to finish my story about the Montana 10-pointer. My arrow cut the femoral artery, and the buck ran only 50 yards. He pitched off a bank and into a river. Had a buddy and I not followed all that blood immediately and spotted the deer bobbing away down the riffles, I'd have lost that big dude. Sometimes it pays to say to heck with it and look hard and fast for a buck if you find blood by the buckets and you're hunting near water.

Deer-Finding Tips:

➤ Even when a shot looks and feels perfect, don't get ahead of yourself. If you don't see a buck go down, you might trail 50 to 75 yards and look for sign. But if you have the slightest inkling that the deer might not be lying dead within 100 yards, back out, chill out and replay the shot in your mind until you get your confidence back. It never hurts to wait several hours to trail a buck, even one that you eventually find shot through both lungs. Better safe than sorry!

➤ After the shot, listen as a buck bolts off in the cover. Cracking sticks, clattering rocks, sloshing water, etc. will help you pattern the route the deer fled. Music to your ears is hearing a big deer fall and expire!

➤ Watch a buck run as far as you can see him. In open country, follow him with your binocular. At the spot where you lose the buck, pick a prominent marker — an oddly shaped tree, big rock, fence post, etc. Climb down from your stand, walk straight to the marker and flag it before you forget it. Take a compass reading to determine the line the deer went.

➤ Go back to the point of impact and examine the cut hair and blood on the ground, or on your arrow if you find it. After determining where you hit the deer, walk back out to your marker and begin trailing. That way you don't waste time between the hit spot and your marker.

➤ Look for blood not only on the ground, but also high on brush, weeds, trees or logs. You might see a streak of blood from an exit hole 2 feet off the ground.

➤ Look well to the sides of a blood trail. A deer might have leapt a log and sprayed blood 3 to 4 feet off to one side of the trail.

➤ If you lose a trail, get down on your hands and knees and look for specks of blood, upturned leaves or stumbling tracks.

➤ As you follow a deer, mark the trail with surveyor's tape. Turn back, study the flags and get

If you hit a deer in the paunch, your arrow might stink. Back off the trail for 8 to 12 hours.

a line on the direction a buck is taking. Keep projecting that line out 50 to 75 yards and look for more blood.

➤ Predict where a deer is headed, maybe to water or a big thicket up ahead, and check that line for sign.

➤ Don't think a buck won't run uphill. I've followed deer that ran straight up ridges and died on the tops.

➤ Check brush piles and dead-falls along a blood trail. A buck might have crawled into a patch of cover and died.

➤ When a buck's running trail (as evidenced by big, wide-spaced, dirt-flinging tracks with blood spraying off to the sides) slows to a walk (the stride of the prints gets noticeably shorter and drops and specks of blood fall straight down to the ground) stop and back out of the area. Chances are the deer is looking for a spot to lie down. Give it a few hours, come back and you're apt to find your deer dead in a bed.

➤ Move slowly and quietly on a blood trail, almost like you're stalking a buck. You never want to jump a wounded animal because he can run a long way on adren-aline alone. If his blood clots, you'll lose the trail.

➤ Only you and one buddy should trail a buck. You don't want an army of guys making noise, putting down scent and stumbling over specks of blood or tracks.

Look for blood not only on the ground, but also high on grass or brush.

➤ The buddy that accompa-nies you on a blood trail should have tremen-dous eyesight and be a good woodsman. He should be able to slip easily through the woods, know what sign to look for and have a knack for detecting blood. He should under-stand how deer react when hit with an arrow.

➤ If you're tracking and hear a deer crash off, stop, listen and get a line on the direction he fled. You might get lucky and hear him fall.

➤ You might hear a deer breathing or gurgling in a thicket up ahead. Stop and don't push it! There's a good chance the buck's lungs are fill-ing up with blood; maybe you made a high lung shot or one-lunged him. Back out of the area and wait a few hours. Chances are the deer will be right there dead.

➤ Sometimes a wounded deer, especially one shot in the paunch, will run off, lie down, feel uncomfortable, get up, move 50 to 100 yards and lie down again. If you don't push that buck, he'll probably die in the second or third bed.

➤ You might follow good blood for 200 yards ... then the trail runs dry. Sometimes a buck will stop bleeding and go on a death run for 40 or 50 yards. Check those last yards for tracks or tiny specks of blood that lead to the buck.

➤ If you think you made a mediocre hit, leave a buck overnight if the weather is cool. But if it's hot or if rain or snow is in the forecast, you'll have to push the envelope. Also, if there are a lot of coyotes or other predators in your area, go ahead and track that buck.

➤ You can gut a buck with a penknife or a Bowie blade. But to do the job right, get your hands on a multi-blade knife designed for deer hunters. Buck, Gerber, Case and other cutlery manufacturers sell sheath models with three or more blades. Use the guthook or blunt-nosed dressing blade to open a deer without worry of piercing the paunch. A small saw blade can be used for splitting a deer's brisket and pelvis, and in a pinch, you can use it to trim limbs when hanging a treestand. Both gutting and saw blades save a knife's main edge—a trailing, drop or clip point on most models—for skinning and the tedious work of caping a trophy buck.

➤ Carry a breakdown, T-style or folding game saw in your pack. A sharp saw that cuts on the push or pull is great for splitting a deer's

There's no finer feeling than popping over a ridge and finding your buck!

brisket and pelvis. Use it to saw the antlers off a buck. And, of course, a saw comes in handy for cutting limbs when hanging a perch or trimming shooting lanes around a stand.

Chapter 10

Northeastern Whitetails

NEIL DOUGHERTY'S first encounter with the buck was near The Hole, a steep, rough-and-tumble spot that he and his friends have rarely hunted over the years. He was out scouting one crisp November day, and when he spotted the wide rack moving in the cover, he sucked a deep breath and whispered to himself, "Whoa, that's the biggest deer I've ever seen on this property." Dougherty wanted to hunt the buck, but he didn't want to spook him. Rather than piling into The Hole, he and his buddies set a few stands on the downwind perimeter of the cover.

From one of those posts a few days later, Neil watched the buck sneak out of The Hole. "His nose was glued to the ground, and by his body language and demeanor you could tell he had a bad case of does on the brain." The animal glided through some oaks and beechnuts, hit a clover-lined logging road and approached a shooting hole 30 yards away. As the brute slipped behind a mass of wild grapes, Dougherty drew. His release was smooth and the arrow hit with a reassuring *thwack*.

He waited until he could stand it no longer, then climbed down and

"The first week to 10 days of bow season in October give you a great opportunity to kill a big Northern buck," says Neil Dougherty.

found his aluminum arrow covered in crimson. Some 75 yards up the blood trail, he spotted a side of brown and then an antler sticking up. Smiling, he ran to the 136-inch buck that lay still in the leaves.

For Neil, that P&Y buck was the pinnacle of success after eight years of intensive game and habitat management on his 500-acre property in western New York. It is the type of quality animal you can take with a bow if you manage and hunt a tract smartly anywhere in the Northeast.

Northern Habitats

With new housing developments, roads, golf courses and the like springing up across the populous Northeast, especially along the Atlantic Coast, more and more lands are being carved into smaller and smaller checkerboard habitats. You might find the remnants of old farms with abandoned fields, orchards and fencerows. There are plenty of brush lots and pockets and strips of timber, often literally in the backyards of new homes. These modern habitats, many of which are only 20 to 200 acres in size, hold lots of whitetails and lots of good bucks. No doubt more P&Y trophies roam the Northeast than ever before.

Dougherty's 500-acre woodland property in Steuben County, New York, is atypical of the aforementioned lands. But it is quite representative of the larger all-woods environments you'll find in other parts of the Northeast, from rural Pennsylvania to western New York and up into Maine.

In either habitat large or small, timbered or broken, the key to bowhunting Northern bucks is to key on their food sources. Prepping for the mid-November rut, as well as the long, harsh winter that is sure to follow, whitetails eat ravenously to pack on fat in September and October. Once the mating season is history, does and bucks seek out whatever scraps of feed they can find to survive till spring.

"Up here deer eat corn and other grains when and

When bucks vanish from food plots in October, look for them rubbing and scraping around oak or beechnut trees where does have moved to feed.

where they have access to them," notes Dougherty. "But in the big woodland habitats, you need to hone in on browse and mast. White oak acorns are the best, but we have lots of soft mast too. For example, many trees in old orchards planted back in the 1930s or 40s still make some fruit. You can never go wrong setting up near those trees early in the season."

For a decade, Dougherty has heavily managed his land. He's planted food plots and strips, cut trees to let in sunlight and grow more browse and fertilized select oak and apple trees. Primarily by increasing the tonnage of green forage on his property, he's gone from seeing spindly 4- and 6-pointers to tagging mature bucks that score 120, 130 and higher. "Get into management and you can greatly improve your hunting too, wherever you live and no matter the size of your land," he says. You'll read about Neil's innovative habitat techniques in Chapter 14.

Scouting

The New Yorker scouts a bunch in cold, snowy January, often while out hunting rabbits or ruffed grouse with his yellow Lab. He covers lots of ground, and he

Dougherty plants plots of Biologic Green Patch a few weeks before archery season. "Those plants grow fast and lush and attract lots of does and bucks," he says.

piles into many covers that at other times he wouldn't.

"We designate about 50 percent of our land as sanctuaries for does and bucks," notes Dougherty. These thick, rough, often steep and rocky covers are scattered across his property, and during most of the year, they are off-limits to scouting, hunting or any other human intrusion. But in the winter, Neil dives into the thickets and looks for sign, most notably major trails and last fall's big rubs.

Finding buck sign is good and exciting, but Dougherty says it's pretty much useless until you start piecing together and analyzing the clues. "Most importantly, I evaluate sign and try to visualize how a buck traveled through an area in relation to the predominant winds back in the fall. Where did his rub lines go and come according to the cover and nearby food plots and oak ridges? Why and how *exactly* did a buck walk that trail?"

As you piece together a buck's pattern, figure he walked and worked into the wind, or at least into a crosswind. Use a compass and consult an aerial photograph to further narrow his moves. That same buck, or another one like him, will travel similarly through the area next fall if food sources and security covers remain unchanged.

Dougherty is consumed with whitetails. He keeps looking for any and all sign as he cuts timber and plants and fertilizes plots and strips in spring and early summer. But after that, his woods scouting is pretty much done. He hangs back on late-summer evenings and glasses his green, lush, fast-growing plots for a shooter to go after during opening week.

Early Tactics

Archery season begins October 15 in New York, and Neil is ready and raring to go. "The first week to 10 days are probably your best opportunity to kill a big Northern deer. The animals are still locked into summer feeding patterns, and if you did your homework and glassing, you know where they are and how they move. Also, you're after bucks that haven't been hunted in almost a year. That's a tremendous advantage."

Neil's number one tactic is to climb into a tree stand on the edge of a Biologic Green Patch plot he planted

Use a map and compass to pattern a buck. Figure he works into the wind or a crosswind when he approaches a food plot.

This super-fresh rub and another five or six like it tell you a buck is running this bottom. Run your stand up a tree where you can see well and there's a good chance you'll see that deer.

only a few weeks ago. "Those plants grow fast and lush and are extremely palatable to deer. They attract a bunch of animals."

If you start the season on unmanaged ground with few or no food plots, try Plan B. Hang a stand on the edge of a cornfield where you glassed a good buck in the summer. Or set up near a recently cut hayfield or pasture where deer are coming to eat succulent green weeds and forbs that just sprouted up. It's a great bow tactic, but one that is overlooked by most hunters across the country. On an all-woods tract, hunt from a tree downwind of acorns or apples. Whatever the case, hunt a lot, especially in the evenings, because now is a reliable time to see and shoot a 120- to 130-class animal.

Everything Dougherty does, from laying out food plots to hanging tree stands on the edges of them, is based on the predominant winds in his Northern area. He points out that those breezes tend to change as bow season rolls on, blowing out of the southeast in early October and shifting around to the west and/or north in November and December. As deer move to and from food plots, acorn flats and other feeding areas, they

tweak their patterns to take advantage of those changing winds, and so should you.

The New York pro monitors the breeze each day and chooses a stand that he can approach and hunt somewhere downwind of where a buck will likely travel and end up to feed. He circles and sneaks through woods where he shouldn't jump a single animal. Then he climbs into a perch smack on the edge of plot. This is in contrast to many Northerners who prefer to sit 50 yards or farther back in the woods off a field, feeling that is where they are most apt to whack a monster before nightfall.

I should point out that Dougherty's plots are not your run-of-the-mill green patches. They are designed, configured and planted specifically with archery hunting in mind. They're small, less than an acre, with nooks, crannies and necks that taper deer movement. You can shoot an arrow across them in places. The pro even builds windrows behind his stands to block deer from circling downwind, in effect forcing the animals to enter a plot off to one side upwind. So his plan is to hunt smack on top of the greens with the odds in his favor.

Northeastern Whitetails

Don't just look for rubbed trees. A buck with testosterone surging in his veins will thrash fence posts, vines or whatever.

from the boys. It can be pretty dead in the woods.

"If you need to catch up on some work, it's a good time to do it," says Neil. He stays out of his best spots and stands, not wanting to lay down scent or spook deer that aren't going to move well anyway. "I might hunt around some acorns on an out-of-the-way ridge a couple of afternoons, but I don't force things."

More often than not during the lull, you'll find Dougherty moving around and glassing fields, plots, logging roads and cut strips of timber from afar. "When I see the first 1½- or 2½-year-old buck chasing a doe, peak breeding is not on yet, but it can happen any day." He makes a beeline back to one of his best stands in an area where he's been spotting a dandy buck.

You'll read more about all this in Chapter 14.

By the middle of archery season, whitetails have eaten much of the greenery in his Green Patch Plus plots, and that is okay by Dougherty. "As the season progresses, I pull off those plots and concentrate my efforts deeper in the woods anyway."

The Lull

At some point in October—*poof*—you might go from seeing 10 to 20 deer in a field or plot in the afternoons to observing half that many animals and no shooter bucks. You probably haven't messed up. "It's just that the midseason lull is on and the hunting gets tough," explains Dougherty.

In late October or even early November some years, typically a week or two prior to the peak of the breeding season, Northern whitetails seem to disappear for a while. Bucks have bulked up and are lying low in thickets, putting on their game faces for the imminent rut. Does are not quite ready to breed, and they're hiding

Rut Tactics

On morning hunts in early to mid-November, Neil hunts a stand that overlooks a ridge, hollow, draw, creek drainage or other transition zone near a doe-bedding area. His afternoon posts are carefully situated well downwind of plots with the best green feed.

Once bow season has been open a month, and once the does begin coming into heat, the New Yorker finds that mature bucks in his part of the world are more adept than ever at circling downwind of plots, smelling for gals out in the fields or scent-checking the trails they walked on earlier in the afternoon. To take advantage of the buck behavior, Neil now hunts from posts 100 to 200 yards downwind of a plot. (By the way, most of those stands were hung back in the summer or early fall.) "Specifically, I like to hunt the first head or point of thick cover downwind of a plot. One afternoon a mature buck is likely to circle right through there, so that's where I put a tree stand."

Like many archers, Dougherty believes your first sit is best for seeing and maybe sticking a giant. Each day thereafter, you swirl more scent and make more noise on the walk in and out of an area. "When a big deer gets on to you, he won't leave the area, but he'll skirt your stand and circle farther and farther downwind of a feeding area as he checks for does."

Okay, so after hunting a stand for a day or two, Neil tries to stay a step ahead of a good buck doing that. "I sneak back to a second stand I hung 60 to 80 yards deeper in the cover and wait for the deer to slip up. I might move three or four times farther and farther back in the woods in hopes of finally getting a shot at him." Again, he tries to hunt the first point of thick cover near those stands, most of which were preset in advance of bow season.

During the rut, try hanging your stands 100 to 200 yards downwind of food plots. You should spot bucks scent-checking for does and sniffing their trails.

Late Strategies

When mid to late December rolls around in the Northeast, temperatures drop steadily into the teens or single digits, and the ice and snow begin to fly and pile up. The conditions will stay harsh for the next three months or so. It's tough on both whitetails and bowhunters.

While a mini second rut occurs in the Mid-Atlantic and New England states around December 10 to 15, most mature bucks turn from rutting to just surviving. The big boys lost 20 to 30 percent of their body weight chasing and breeding does last month. Their instincts tell them they've got to eat. Around a late food source is where you might yet stick a big deer if you can handle the cold.

"A secret weapon in the North is the brassica plant," says Dougherty, who sows some Biologic Maximum brassica plots across his property specifically for late-season hunting. He points out that whitetails might walk right through the big, tall, leafy plants in early fall without taking a nibble. But when frost and snow cause a chemical reaction that turns the starches in the brassicas to sugar, deer, and especially bucks, love them.

"After the rut, you're liable to find our does scattered out and feeding all over the place because they want to be away from the bucks," notes the pro. "The good news is that you might spot eight to 10 bucks in one of your brassica plots each day."

The more brutal the weather, the better. Anytime Dougherty gets four or five straight days of bitter cold

When it's cold and snowy, Dougherty hangs tough in one of his best stands near a food source. "I can handle the conditions because I anticipate seeing several bucks and getting a shot at a big one," he says.

and snow with northwest winds, he bundles up and sits a stand on the southeast (downwind) side of one of his Maximum plots. "I can handle the conditions because I go with the anticipation of seeing multiple bucks and getting a shot at a big one. The bucks have to eat."

At the tag end of bow season, it pays to get on stand early in the afternoon, by 2 o'clock or so. Also, try hunting around food plots or crop fields or just back in the nearby timber in the morning as well. "Bucks feed some in the wee hours, but I find they lay up on really cold nights, not wanting to expend unnecessary energy," says Dougherty. They often get up and move to the feed when it's sunniest and warmest during the mid-morning and mid-afternoon hours. That's when you need to be out there.

Since many Northern bucks feed and yard up in brassica plots throughout the winter, these are prime bone-hunting grounds. "I find some sheds in the sanctuaries, but I pick up most of them in my Maximum plots," notes Neil. "One year I found nine perfect sets in a ³/₄-acre plot. It was pretty awesome."

With that, Dougherty's hunting comes full circle. Those sheds give him a good idea of how many local bucks, and which big deer, survived the previous bow and gun season. If those bucks make it through the rest of the winter and don't get hit by a car over the summer, some to most of them should be back on his land next fall, wearing even larger racks.

Plant some brassicas for late-season hunting. When the cold and snow turn the big, leafy plants sugary, deer love them.

Northern Tips:

➤ Whitetails love a diverse menu. In addition to clover, grains and mast, they browse a bunch. Scout for browse strips, especially those rimming food plots or oak ridges or bottoms, and hang tree stands nearby. In West Virginia, Maryland and Pennsylvania, deer browse greenbrier, blackberry and honeysuckle a lot. Dougherty points out that farther north, the top five browse species for whitetails are apple, basswood, ash, aspen and hard maple. Whitetails feed heavily on white cedar and hemlock in wintertime.

➤ Northern deer eat beechnuts when there is a good crop, but that might be only once every seven to 10 years. Check for this mast each fall, "but don't put too much stock in it," notes Dougherty. "Acorns are more reliable, and deer like them better anyway."

➤ When deep snow covers grain fields and green plots in December and January, go back to bowhunting over secondary feed in south- and east-facing woods, where the snow is not so deep. Deer will eagerly paw through the snow to get at apples, cherries, acorns, beechnuts and any other leftover mast they can find.

➤ A heavy, old Northern buck pocks the snow with wide, splayed tracks 3 to 4 inches long (excluding dew claws). Buck prints generally run in a fairly straight line, while doe tracks tend to meander. Note that a buck's stride is longer than a doe's.

Northern deer love to browse. A trail might lead to ash, basswood, apple, aspen or maple.

➤ Across the high North, whitetails flock to cedar or hemlock swamps when the snow flies in winter. A swamp or thicket 20 acres or less is generally easiest to hunt. Hang a bow stand along a track-pocked edge, on a finger ridge or in a gentle draw. Cedars or hemlocks near fields are best, but in a big-woods environment, you'll do best to set up where evergreen and white oak ridges meet.

➤ All you Northern archers might want to monitor the full moons in October and November and plan your hunts accordingly. Whitetail expert Charles Alsheimer, author of *Hunting Whitetails by the Moon* (Krause Publications, 1999), owns hunting and research land a few miles from Dougherty's place in New York. "Alsheimer's predictions on when bucks will move and rut according to the moon each year are pretty much right on the money in our part of the world," Neil notes.

Chapter 11

The South's Tough Bucks

Darrell Daigre scouts as much as he hunts all season long. "We've got more hard-core bowhunters down here in the South than anywhere else in the country," he says. "To kill big deer you need to move around and find spots that don't get too much pressure."

THICK AND HUMID, the predawn wraps you like a wet blanket as you ease to your tree stand deep in the black oaks. The hardwoods shimmer to silver, and turkeys begin clucking and yelping out over a dark-water slough. An old tom tosses out a short gobble; you jump and anticipate the coming spring for a moment. Wood ducks lift from a nearby river and whistle overhead, their wings singing. Shorebirds splash and caw. A barred owl booms one last time that morning. The woods are alive and so are you.

Southern deer either skirt sloughs and swamps or walk right through them in shallow spots. Scout for how and where trails run, and hang your tree stands accordingly.

When the rut busts loose in Dixie, hunt hard during the middle of the day, especially if the moon is full. These guys dragged out this Alabama buck at 1:00 p.m.

Around 7 o'clock, the first doe eases by, her coat tan and slick, her lower legs black from wading the swamps. Another gal slips by, and then three more. Then the action slows, but still you wait.

You peek at your watch. Nine-twenty. Time to bear down and watch and listen. Down here in mid-January, you *expect* to see good bucks on their feet during the sparkling mid-morning hours.

There! The deer moves quickly and with purpose, his hips swaying and his nose working the ground like a Hoover gone mad. Eighty yards out he stops to check the pee trail of a doe. You ease up your binoculars for a good look. The buck is old, short-faced and with a chest the size of a beer keg, and man the symmetry of his antlers! It was as if the Creator made a plaster cast of an impeccable 8-point rack and set it delicately atop the beautiful animal.

The buck, whose bone-white rack you figure scores in the high 120s, keeps coming. When he slides behind a hackberry tree, you raise your bow. Another five steps and the critter will be broadside at 20 yards in the best shooting hole down to your left.

He stops. The wind is perfect, and no way he saw you draw. The deer turns and peels farther off to the left, as if pulled over there by some mysterious and unknown force. You let down and watch him disappear into the swamp. You shake your head and manage a dry half-smile. What they say is right: These Southern bucks are the toughest whitetails in the world to bow hunt.

Southern whitetails can smell you a mile away or look up, bust you in a tree stand and come unglued. Kill a thick-racked buck with your bow and you've earned it.

First Season

"There are two good times to hunt our deer, either the first week of bow season or two or three months later during the rut," says Darrell Daigre of West Point, Mississippi. "The rut in December or January is the most exciting time to be in the woods, but depending on where you hunt, the first or second week of October can be just as good or even better. I've shot most of my mature bucks early."

Big, fresh rubs on the edge of a swamp or pine plantation tell you at least one good buck is bedding nearby.

the first four or five days of the Alabama bow season, so I double my chances of scoring early and big."

The early-fall hunting is awesome because like in other parts of the country, bucks are still in bachelor groups and still on predictable bed-to-feed patterns. But you'd better try to stick a good deer quickly. "The first four or five days of archery season are about the only time our deer are patternable to some extent," notes Daigre. "After that, they start to feel the human intrusion and their routines start to fall apart. We have a lot of hard-core bowhunters down here, as many or more as anywhere in the country, and they hit it hard from October till the end of the season."

That constant pressure is the main reason an old swamp buck is the toughest whitetail on the planet to kill with a bow.

Daigre starts his serious scouting in September, looking for bachelor groups with one or two of the best shooters. Many of the areas he hunts, especially lands in south Alabama, are flat and wet. He can't climb a mountain or bluff and glass down onto fields for deer like guys in other parts of the country do. So in the evenings, he simply drives around in his truck and checks food plots with his binoculars and spotting scope. Many mornings, he goes back out at first light and checks for deer moving off the plots, or easing across a hay field or clearcut in the summer haze en route to a bedding area back in the woods or a swamp.

Says Daigre, "You never know when or where you'll spot a big deer and learn a piece of his pattern, so it pays to observe a lot. Spend hours glassing, and look in many different places. You need to find where a shooter is living as best you can. Then play the wind, sneak in, hang a stand and try to make it happen in a day or two. After the first week, you might not see another good deer till the rut in mid-December or January."

The good news is that in early October, single shooters or clubs of three or four 120- to 140-class bucks often enter and leave a crop field or food plot in the same gen-

If you're lucky, you'll have a couple of places to hunt in a couple of different states when bow season rolls around. Daigre hunts in Mississippi, where bow season opens October 1, and also in Alabama, where the season starts October 15. "That gives me the opportunity to hunt the first four or five days near home and then

This Alabama buck dogged a doe beneath my tree stand one afternoon during the last week of January. Hunting the latest rut in the U.S. is fun!

eral area, sometimes even walking the same trail that wends out of a pine plantation or swamp. Daigre hangs a stand right on the edge of the feeding area in hopes of hitting the jackpot.

Like whitetails everywhere, Southern critters are habitual. "Often I find myself hunting the same sets from previous years," continues the Mississippi pro. "But, of course, sometimes a big deer will throw you a curve and pop out into a plot 100 to 200 yards away, so you need to be flexible and ready to readjust stands from day to day."

As in most parts of the country, the early-October hunting down South is pretty much an afternoon gig. Some mornings Daigre hunts an offbeat transition zone between a food source and a bedding area, but he never forces things in an area where he thinks he might stick a big deer one evening. "The first week I rarely go into my best spots in the mornings. Why risk scenting up the woods, jumping deer and changing a good buck's pattern?"

In a perfect world near his home in Mississippi, Daigre would hunt like a wild man from October 1 to 5, and then stay completely out of his best spots until the rut busted loose in mid-December. These days you'd be hard pressed to find a piece of Southern woods that doesn't receive at least some hunting pressure in late October and November. The truth is, most places get pounded. "But if guys could just condition themselves to stay out of their best spots till the rut, their archery hunting would be so much better," points out the pro. "They'd see a lot more mature bucks and get more shots at 'em. It all comes back to the pressure."

During the long midseason lull, which in the South runs from late October through November and even December in some places, old bucks seem to go underground and Daigre goes back to work. But the deer fanatic can't help but to play some days. "I generally bowhunt back in the woods near falling acorns or other mast now." Many mornings and afternoons he drives around and glasses and observes whatever might be

Daigre loves to hunt the rut, but he's killed more good bucks near food plots during opening week of the Alabama and Mississippi bow seasons.

This Virginia buck didn't have an enormous rack, but he was 4-1/2 years old and a real trophy for the high-pressured lease I hunted. I shot him prowling for a doe at 11:30 a.m.

going on with the herds in his areas. But he stays out of his best spots as much as he can. The second best season, the wild and crazy winter rut, will be here before you know it.

The Southern Rut

It's fascinating how the Southern rut varies from state to state, from region to region and even from locale to locale. From Virginia to Kentucky to northern Georgia, bucks corral and breed does in mid-November, as they do in most parts of the country. Near Daigre's home in eastern Mississippi, however, deer typically rut from around December 10 through Christmas. On delta lands south and west in Mississippi and Louisiana, the

peak is around December 18. In parts of central Alabama, the deer go wild in early January, and 80 miles or so south, the rut goes off around January 16.

This long, late and scattergun rut offers a unique opportunity for Dixie sportsmen. "If you have several properties scattered in different areas of a couple of states, within say a 150-mile radius, you could hunt the rut from early December through the end of January," says Daigre. "That would obviously be fun, and it would give you a great chance of killing a couple of big deer each year."

Another cool thing is how the South's rut kicks in virtually overnight. "One day in December or January, there's nothing in the woods expect a few old deer tracks," notes the pro. "Then it's like somebody threw a switch and *boom*, the trees and ground are all torn up."

Deer in the Deep South tend to rub and scrape as much or more than bucks in other parts of the U.S. "They rub all types of trees, but they really love to thrash pines and especially big cedars," notes Daigre. The pro is always on the lookout for those sweet-smelling signposts, or what he calls community rubs.

There is scientific support for doing so. Noted whitetail biologist Dr. Grant Woods believes bucks $3\frac{1}{2}$ years of age and older blaze thick trees repeatedly during a single fall and re-rub some of them year after year. "Our research suggests signpost rubs play a critical role in the social dynamics of a deer herd." Woods points out that mature bucks deposit pheromones on the rubs. When does come by and inhale the scent-based, airborne chemicals, it may affect the timing of their estrus, perhaps causing them to "come in" earlier than normal. Also, pheromones send a powerful signal to young bucks to let them know their place is near the bottom rung of the buck hierarchy.

Although only older bucks shred signposts, all deer interact with them, looking at, smelling or walking up to touch the rubs. "They act as communal pheromone wicks and as such are usually located in areas with high deer traffic," says Woods. Look for mega rubs along a brushy edge, on a hogback ridge or in a similar spot that might funnel deer. Hang a tree stand nearby and watch for Mr. Big cruising the area.

The bucks are also scraping fiends, as I found out not long ago on an Alabama hunt with Daigre. That January afternoon he dropped me off and pointed to my tree stand at the far end of a BioLogic plot. As I snuck along the south edge of the field, I noticed a couple of scrapes. It looked as though a buck, and probably more than one, had hit them within the day, though it was tough to tell in the sandy soil. Anyhow, the farther I walked, the more scrapes I saw. By the time I reached my perch 300 yards away, I had walked past 28 freshly pawed scrapes, with some only 10 yards apart! Surely some of that pawing was the work of young bucks, but I reckoned that at least one stud had hit some of the scrapes too. Maybe it was the barrel-chested 8-pointer that chased a doe past my stand and across that scrape line later that afternoon.

I didn't get a shot at that big deer, but at least I was in his world. That pretty much sums up Daigre's rut strategy. When a mother lode of rubs and scrapes pop up in a spot, he figures at least one good buck is at work there. He plays the wind, moves in, hangs a tree stand amid all the sign and bowhunts the spot *right now.*

"You can see a lot of good bucks back in early October, but it's my experience that you don't see the four-, five- or six-year-old giants until the rut pops in December or January, depending on where you're hunting," says the pro. "And then you might have only three or four days to see and hunt a big one before he goes

underground again or the season closes. So go after a good deer where he's living and rubbing and scraping and looking for does. Sit your stand all day if you can hack it, because you might see him anytime."

When the heavy chasing starts, one of Daigre's favorite tactics is to drive or still-hunt around, glassing for deer rutting in fields, plots or clear-cuts. "If I can spot a good buck chasing a doe, I sneak into the area and run a climbing stand up a tree. You've got to play the wind, but I've found that rut-wild deer don't pay much attention to any walking noise you make. More times than not, I end up smack in the middle of the action. Sometimes I even spot several bucks after one hot doe. Again, I'm in the game."

On days when the rut is happening but he can't spot any chases, the pro reverts to the old strategy of "hunting the does" because the bucks will be somewhere close. But down South, you hunt the does with a twist.

On another Alabama hunt a few years ago, Daigre and I were sitting in Portland Lodge one night, lamenting our fate. It was January 18 and the rut was full tilt, but neither of us was having much luck. "I didn't even see a doe this afternoon," I moaned.

Joe Champion, who has been head guide and land manager at Portland for decades, overheard my whining and asked, "You been hunting food plots?"

"Yep, good ones, too," I replied.

"No wonder you aren't seeing any deer," Joe drawled and chuckled.

Champion went on to tell me that when the rut erupts in south Alabama, does hightail it out of fields, food plots and other open areas. "They don't want bucks chasing them all over the place, so they dive into thick cover to hide. Heck, you can watch a food plot for days and not see a deer."

With that in mind, Daigre has devised a new rut strategy. Many days, he simply heads to a pine plantation, thick clear-cut or weed field where he figures some does are hiding from bucks. He runs a climber up a tree downwind of the cover and looks and listens. "You never know what you might see or hear—deer chasing and crashing around, a buck grunting or even two bucks sparring. If you're lucky, a hot doe tired of being harassed in the close quarters will pop out of the cover with a big buck on her heels. Now getting those deer within bow range and then stopped for a shot is a challenge. But at least you're into deer and you've got a chance."

Hunting downwind of thick cover and rutting deer begs the question: Shouldn't you rattle or grunt? "Sometimes, definitely," says Daigre, who goes on to point out that he has been hunting in the South all his life, and he just rattled up his first buck in January of 2004. Actually, he rattled up several bucks that crisp morning, including a fine 8-pointer that skirted his stand

at 70 yards. It is telling to note that several other hunters in camp also rattled up multiple deer during that magical 3-day span.

"It is my opinion that rattling and grunting can work here in the South when the rut is on and the bucks are in just the right mood to respond," says Daigre. "But your timing has to be perfect. Really, it involves a lot of trial and error. If you see a buck and rattle at him and he comes unglued and runs the other way, obviously your timing is off."

In that case, it would be a good idea to go back to hunting stealthily and quietly, which is best most days in the South. But keep your horns and calls handy and try them during the next little span when the bucks are running wild again.

Daigre believes that rattling and grunting don't work as consistently well in the Southeast as they do in, say, Texas or Iowa because of the extremely high deer densities in states like Mississippi and Alabama. Also, the sex ratio of most Southern herds is skewed toward too many females. "We have so many deer that oftentimes when you rattle or grunt, I believe you scare the heck out of young deer close by. Those deer come unglued, run and spook all the deer in the area. So instead of coming your way, a buck follows their lead and goes the other way."

Due in large part to the high deer densities and big number of does across the Southeast, the rut here is not as short and intense as in states like Kansas, Iowa or Illinois. "Down here in December or January, you might have three or four days when the deer are running wide open, and then they shut down overnight," points out Daigre. "Three or four days later bucks start chasing like mad again for two or three days

After rattling to a buck, watch his reaction. If he runs away, your timing is off, so keep quiet. If he looks and walks your way, get ready!

before the woods go quiet again. It goes on like that for a while. You just never know."

But the Mississippi archer knows one thing. "When things are right and the big bucks are scraping and chasing, our bowhunting is as fun and exciting as you'll find anywhere in the country."

Southern Tips:

> The mosquitoes can be horrific on a hot, humid afternoon in October, especially if your stand is set near a still slough or swamp. Wear a couple layers of lightweight shirts and pants, a neck gaiter and a facemask. Spray down with a scent-free, DEET-based repellent like Scent Shield's No Stinking Bugs. "Most days you can handle it," says Daigre, "but if the bugs are too bad one day, you might want to stay out of your best stand so you won't move and swipe too much and spook a lot of deer."

> Climbing stands are popular in the South, where there are tons of straight pine and hardwood trees. Learn to use one safely, and then climb frequently all season near where bucks rub, scrape or chase does. You'll get more shots at more big bucks by being flexible and mobile.

> Don't let the sandy soil fool you. Tracks and scrapes in sand are generally fresher than they look.

> I've found that in the Deep South warm, humid weather doesn't necessarily shut down deer movement like it does farther north. Heck, if the whitetails never moved in a 70-degree soup, they often wouldn't eat for weeks! But frosty, clear, high-pressure days in December or January are hard to top. "Under those conditions, you might spot a good buck moving any time of day," notes Daigre.

Southern hunters love their climbers. Use one to move around and hunt where bucks feed, rub, scrape and chase does.

> Lacrosse's calf-high rubber boots are to the swamps and river bottoms what Nikes are to the hoops court. Rubbers or high-topped leather boots lined with Supprescent not only keep your feet dry, they also knock down your scent and keep red bugs, ticks and other pests out.

➤ Check the edges of swamps and sloughs for fresh tracks and trails. Bucks sometimes stop to rub cypress trees or knees. Hang a stand downwind of a hot water crossing and you'll see whitetails.

➤ Say one evening you glass a food plot and spot an old buck with black lower legs. That deer is spending a lot of time around or crossing a nearby slough or swamp. Check an aerial and hang a stand on a ridge or in a draw that leads back to his watery travel corridor or bedding cover.

➤ In many areas, rising and falling rivers and creeks determine a lot of the deer movement. Monitor water levels and set your bow stands accordingly. For example, if a food plot, oak bottom or thicket becomes flooded, deer will probably hop over to the next closest feeding or bedding area. Set up over there and try to surprise a buck.

➤ Check out 3- to 5-year-old pine plantations. They offer plenty of cover for pressured deer, but enough sunlight still filters through to grow honeysuckle and other green browse. A pine thicket near a crop field or food plot will hold the most animals. A good trick is to hang a stand in a nearby hardwood or mature pine where you can see up and down a good number of rows. Watch for bucks coming, going or browsing.

Check a creek or swamp for fresh tracks and rubs. Hang a stand downwind of a water crossing and you'll see deer.

➤ How does the full moon in December or January impact the Southern rut? I don't believe it causes does to come into estrus or otherwise kicks off the breeding season, but I can say this much from my experiences: From Louisiana to Alabama, some of the best rutting activity you'll experience anywhere can occur from 10:00 a.m. till 3:00 p.m. when a full moon overlaps the peak breeding days. You might see and shoot a Southern monster on the prowl or chasing a gal during this time, so be out there!

111

Chapter 12

Monsters of the Midwest

"Sign is good, but nothing beats glassing a shooter," says Dan Perez. "Besides, long-range scouting lets you study a buck and his movements without leaving your scent all over his living room."

OCTOBER **10, 2003.** It was Dan Perez's first hunt of the year, and he slipped through the timber with some mighty high expectations. The Illinois archer had picked a stand based on multiple late-summer observations. He knew of two huge bucks that were gorging on some winter wheat he'd planted earlier. Hopefully, he'd get a good, close look at one of them.

The southeast breeze was perfect for the evening's hunt. Perez played that wind and snuck to his stand without bumping a single deer. So far, so good. He climbed up, roped up his bow and sat for three long, slow hours. Other than a couple does and a yearling buck off in the distance, not many critters stirred.

An hour before sundown, the timber dimmed and cooled. The hunter shivered as he caught sight of a huge-bodied buck dogging a doe through a bottom 300 yards away. "I'd know that thick rack anywhere," Perez remembers thinking. It was one of the monsters he'd spotted in the summer.

Even at that distance, it was plain to see the doe was not impressed by the dominant buck's early courtship advances. She'd scamper a ways and then slow down to browse; he followed along dutifully, nose down and sniffing. All the hunter could do was sit and wait and hope the gal would eventually lead the stud his way.

Perez has killed several Illinois monsters by hunting near remote waterholes during hot, dry ruts. Chasing deer get thirsty and have to drink, so play off that weakness when you can.

It was a long shot, but amazingly, with 15 minutes of shooting light left, the doe turned and came his way. The buck trailed some 60 seconds behind her. Perez ranged the doe at 42-yards as she passed through his shooting window. When the barrel-chested brute reached that same point a minute later, he unleashed a Carbon Force arrow. Not long after that, he sat holding the antlers of his latest trophy, a massive, tall-tined 9-pointer that scored 166 inches and change.

Early October

"Low impact is the key to my early-season success," says Perez. He glasses crop fields, food plots and travel corridors near those feeding areas from afar, trying to locate mature bucks without wasting valuable time sitting in spots where no big deer roam. "Sign is good, but nothing beats seeing a shooter," he notes. "Besides, long-range scouting lets me study a buck and his habits without leaving my scent all over his living room."

Once the Illinois pro has a fairly good handle on a buck's pattern, he slips in one afternoon and hangs a stand. "By a fairly good handle, I mean I know a good buck is coming to a particular food source. Exactly when and where is still somewhat speculative at this point."

In October, deer bed close—tighter than most bowhunters think—to crop fields, food plots and oak flats. For fear of bumping bedded animals, Perez hangs a few tree stands on the outer fringes of popular feeding areas. "That way I can keep an eye on what's going in an area and adapt my location if necessary without spooking any deer."

Choosing the right wind on which to hunt a food source is always iffy and a balancing act. "Ideally, I prefer a crosswind, where my scent is blown away from a buck's approach route and toward part of a field where I don't expect to see deer while I'm on stand," says the pro.

Like many seasoned archers, Perez believes your first time on stand offers your best chance at a mega buck, but he doesn't count on it. "I try to position my stands where I can observe the largest number of deer coming to a food source without one of them winding or seeing me. I feel like every time a deer, buck or doe, catches you on stand, you've reduced your chances of harvesting a mature animal from that location. You've affected the herd's behavioral pattern. Whitetails will not leave an area completely, but they'll sure begin to circumvent your stand."

The thing Perez likes most about the first week of October is that you're after game that hasn't been jumped or otherwise hassled since last hunting season. "It's an excellent time to catch a big Midwestern buck off guard and one of my favorite times to hunt."

Perez cracks his horns once or twice and hangs them up. "I believe that if a buck hears your rattles, he knows where you are," he says. "It might take 20 minutes or 2 hours, but he might come in if you're still and patient."

The Pre-Rut

From Missouri to Michigan to Illinois, the rubbing and scraping phase of the pre-rut kicks off in mid to late October and runs through early November. Mature bucks start to move more and more, smelling and looking for does.

"Where I hunt, an old buck may cover 10 to 15 miles a day as he checks on does," notes Perez. "That's a big change when you consider that during the first couple of weeks of the season, bucks traveled only a short ways between bed and feed."

The Illinois pro hones in on hardwood ridges, edges, fencerows and similar funnels where bucks are most likely to travel. He also focuses on primary scrapes and scrape lines. "It's been my experience that many dominant bucks check their scrapes from a good distance downwind. I hang my stands to intercept a giant as he comes through to wind-check a primary scrape or scrape line. Guys tell me all the time about hanging stands 20 yards off hot scrapes only to watch them turn ice cold. Well, more often than not, a big buck wind-checked those hunters along with the scrapes."

Late in the pre-rut, with bucks busting with testosterone and prowling farther than ever, Perez starts rattling and grunting. The fact is calling is his ace in the hole.

The Midwesterner doesn't call just anywhere. He sets up where a buck would be unable to circle his position, or at the very least would have to show himself if

Some rut days, Perez enters the timber at midmorning and sits till dark. By entering and exiting a stand just once a day, you make less noise and leave less scent. You might even spot a huge buck dogging a doe on the hike in.

he tried to hook in downwind, as most big deer do. "A few yards upwind of a steep ledge, creek bank, lake edge, deep hollow or open field—a spot like that is where I like to grunt or rattle."

Perez believes that many hunters never realize they've been smelled and caught by a circling buck. "Also, I think some bucks come in downwind to check things out long after a rattling or grunting hunter has left the woods. The deer get a double nostril of lingering scent. Such schooling makes an already cautious critter

Perez sometimes hangs a stand to overlook a brushy draw or ridge near a doe-bedding thicket. "It's a great way to see a giant on a morning or midday hunt," he says.

that much harder to kill with a bow. Many times, it's better not to rattle at all if your setup is not right."

Whenever possible, the pro sets his stand uphill of where he expects a buck to come from. "While I've had a fair amount of luck rattling in bucks from level ground, it's been my experience that big deer will travel uphill to the sounds of two bucks fighting more often and more eagerly."

Wherever he hunts, Perez rattles and grunts much more sparingly then most people do. He believes that too much calling or rattling is unrealistic and can at times make bucks leery. He also thinks that when a buck hears your rattles or grunts for the first time, he knows

exactly where they came from. "It might take a big deer twenty minutes or a couple of hours, but he might eventually come to check things out if you're patient."

Peak Rut

Across the Midwest, the wild and woolly peak starts around the 10th of November and runs until Thanksgiving, give or take a few days. Now bucks are gaga, completely engrossed in finding receptive does. "Their lusting rage makes them vulnerable," notes Perez.

Two or three weeks prior in the pre-rut, scrapes

were useful in deciphering buck travel. Two or three weeks prior to that, setting up along an active rub-line would have been a good plan of attack. During these earlier periods, bucks were predictable to some extent. Now all bets are off.

"Unfortunately, many hunters don't realize bucks abort their patterns quickly once the does start coming into estrus," says Perez. "Those hunters often fail primarily because they continue to use pre-rut tactics." He goes on to say that now is the time to jettison rub lines and scrapes and concentrate on doe family units. Bucks are hunting doe units and so should you.

Look for does in and around a primary food source, like a cornfield or clover plot or falling acorns back in the timber. Also, try to find thickets, cedar pockets, brushy bottoms and other spots where various doe groups bed.

With doe units located, Perez looks for his number one rut sign, what he calls "chasing tracks." It's a maze of large (buck) and smaller (doe) tracks together in mud or snow. The more the tracks run around and atop one another, the more you can figure there's a hot doe in the area.

As mentioned earlier, the Illinois pro is of the notion that an old titan may cover 10 or more miles in a single day in search of a ready doe. "I believe one of the reasons bucks are most vulnerable during the peak is because their travels often lead them out of their familiar core areas. For a few minutes of ecstasy, many giants leave their 'home court' and roam in search of receptive mates. The lingering aroma of an estrous doe is enough to make a big deer do careless things as he cruises from one doe area to the next."

To ambush a monster on the lam, Perez hangs a few tree stands to overlook funnels, keying on edges, finger ridges and the like that lead toward doe bedding areas. "It's a great plan for morning and mid-day hunts. However, for the evenings I prefer to stand-hunt a connecting funnel closer to a feeding area. Although bucks are more interested in locating hot does than they are in eating, many does are still on feeding patterns, and hence their crazed suitors will be tagging along. That's why it's not uncommon to catch a gigantic buck lusting for an exasperated doe out in the middle of a wide-open field around ten in the morning. During no other time of the season would a mature buck make such a foolish mistake!"

Perez goes on to point out that a funnel is any terrain that narrows whitetail movement. "It would be nice and simple if every deer funnel resembled the perfect hourglass, with a narrow cover strip linking two enormous bodies of timber. But most funnels are a lot more subtle." A low spot in a creek or fence, a strip of dry ground between two sloughs and a hundred other small and seemingly nondescript terrains can taper a buck's travel options.

Although hunting near a water hole is most popular out West, the technique can be effective in the Heartland as well. "If we've had a lack of rain and the peak of the rut is fast approaching, I often head for a watering area in or near a major food source," says Perez, who asks you to picture this:

The rut is in full swing and old Mossy Horns has been running ridges and chasing does in fields all night. As the pink-orange sun peeks over the horizon, many gals filter back through the timber toward their bedding areas. By now, the old buck is worn out from the night's prowl and ready to rest, so he lies down for awhile. Then around 8 a.m., he's back on his feet. With flared nostrils, the giant tests the air for the seductive juices of an estrous doe. Soon he's back at it, moving fast and hard up and down ridges. Temporarily, the gals have given the old boy the slip.

First, a yearling doe wanders down to a secluded pond to get a drink, followed by her twin and then a big doe. Before long, several other deer move down to wet their whistle. Suddenly, the does are alerted once again by the *"urp, urp, urp"* of the lovesick buck. Crunching leaves and cracking sticks confirm he's back again.

Like a raging bull, Old Mossy emerges, and the does scatter like quail. But before continuing the wild pursuit, the buck walks down to the pond's edge for a drink. Suppose you were hanging 20 feet up a tree and 20 yards away?

Secluded watering holes can be great ambush spots during the rut, especially in a hot, dry fall in an area where there are few creeks or ponds in the first place. Chasing bucks and fleeing does need to drink, so play off that weakness if you can.

Although the peak is the shortest of the rut stages in the Midwest, it's the time when the mature bucks are most on their feet during daylight hours. It is a time of maximum exposure for big deer, and consequently, you ought to maximize your time in the timber, too.

"Once you establish a good stand site, the key to success is to stay put," says Perez. "If you can endure spending the entire day on stand, your time will be well invested. If all day is too much, I recommend entering the timber at midmorning and spending the remainder of the day on stand." He explains that by going in late rather than during the predawn, you can see well ahead in the woods and fields, so you're less likely to bump deer along the way. "Also, by entering and exiting the timber just once during the day, you'll leave less scent to

Go the low-impact route late in the season. Glass feeding areas from afar, try to locate and pattern one last buck and move in for the kill.

alert deer. You know, a mature doe or buck only has to make one trip across your scent path to know danger lurks."

The Post-Rut

A second rut normally comes in between the 10th and the 15th of December in the areas Perez hunts. "This late rut is far less intense than the primary rut because there are fewer estrous does in the timber. But some big bucks are still on the prowl, covering lots of ground in daylight hours as they try for one last breeding opportunity. You've still got a good shot."

The pro hunts the first weeks of the post-rut the same way he hunted the primary rut. "I look for those chasing tracks, which are still the hottest sign." He watches funnels, and he keeps banging the horns and grunting sparingly in hopes of reeling in a shooter cruising for a last gal.

When both ruts are pretty much history in mid to late December, it's time to change tactics yet again for the "recuperation period". Late in the season some deer still seize the opportunity to breed one last time. But most worn-out and skinny bucks, having just lost 20 to 30 percent of their body weight, spend their time feeding and then bedding to conserve energy.

"On many properties, feed is limited," notes Perez. "If you can find a crop field or plot with a few grains of nourishment left, that place will draw deer like a magnet." Once again, like in the early season, the pro goes the low-impact route. He glasses feeding areas from afar, tries to locate and pattern one last buck and moves in for the kill.

With just a few days left in the season and a tag still burning in your pocket, Perez says to reach into the bottom of your trick bag. He scours aerial photos for remote spots with a little cover, water and especially a few morsels of food. "Places that received little or no human disturbance during the major part of the season are best." Think a weedy culvert near a back road or an overgrown hog lot behind a barn. You get the idea. A spot like that is where you might get one last crack at a mid-America giant.

Midwestern Tips:

➤ "I've heard hunters claim their new bows are so fast it's impossible for a deer to jump the string," says Perez, who is a sales manager for PSE Archery and a bow-tackle whiz. "But the truth is, within a normal shooting distance of 15 to 40 yards, any quick, keen-eared big critter can get out of the way of an arrow launched from the fastest bow. Sound travels at more than 1,100 fps; a compound with overdraw and shooting light arrows is lucky to clock 300 fps." To quiet your bow and spook fewer deer, Perez advises to tighten your stabilizer, cable guard and every screw on your sight, arrow rest and quiver. Tie on string silencers. Make sure both eccentrics on a two-cam bow are synchronous or "in time." "It's important that you shoot a one-cam bow at peak weight or within four pounds of peak, otherwise you're liable to get a twang from the loose cables and string," he notes. Also, arrow weight, or rather lack of it, can cause a bow to make a loud cracking sound when shot. Optimally, your arrows should weigh at least six grains for every pound of bow weight. The sound an arrow makes when it slides across a rest can easily alert deer. Use Teflon fork tamers, heat shrink or moleskin to cure any problems. Also, pad around your rest with Window Skins or moleskin in case an arrow jumps off the rest when you draw on a buck. Finally, keep the moving parts of your bow well lubed and quiet.

➤ Scout for hedge apples and osage orange as you scout. Near these soft masts you might stick a buck early in the season.

➤ Deep creek banks that cut many parts of the Midwest are perfect for hiding in as you sneak toward a bow stand. "It's also important to establish an avenue that provides the least amount of contact with foliage," adds Perez. "Clipping a few branches and wearing high-top rubber boots can go a long way to reducing your ground scent."

➤ When fronts push in from the north or west in the fall, temperature drops of 30 to 40 degrees or more are not uncommon in Iowa, Kansas and other states. After a warm spell, these extreme drops will get bucks up and moving, so get out there and hunt. Bucks usually move best during the one or two clear, high-pressure days after a cold front blows through. Go get in one of your best stands, even though you might have to deal with a brisk wind.

➤ In the central Midwest's checkerboard habitat of CRP and crop fields, weedy creek bottoms, fencerows and strips and pockets of timber, deer are highly visible and patternable. Glass as much or more than you hunt

To keep from spooking deer, keep your bow lubricated and quiet.

during all weeks of the season. Find a good buck and pin his movements as best you can. When the wind and weather are right, move in and hang a stand for a quick strike.

➤ Look for the narrowest strip of CRP ground between two big blocks of timber, or between corn or soybeans and timber. Hang a stand in a thin point of woods where the wind is right and you'll see a lot of whitetails in that funnel.

➤ A great place for a morning stand in late October or early November is on a long hogback ridge 100 yards or so off a grain field or food plot. Multiple bucks will run that ridge, rubbing, scraping and nosing does as they head for a bedding area each day. Morning thermals will rise and lift your scent away, making the setup even better.

Chapter 13

Bowhunting the West

You'll find some awesome bowhunting in Western river bottoms. It's common to glass 20, 50 or more deer feeding in an alfalfa field at dusk. More than a few of the bucks sport Pope-and-Young racks. Lucas Strommen photo.

IF YOU'VE NEVER HEADED **WEST** for whitetails before, I suggest you pack your bow, arrows and camouflage and go real soon. The endless plains the color of tanned deer hide ... the cottonwood bottoms with the snaking, glinting rivers ... the alfalfa fields that shimmer like giant emeralds in the bright sunshine ... and the soaring, snow-capped mountains off in the distance make the scenery absolutely stunning from one end of the horizon to the other, and it wraps you up.

For the deer hunter from back East or the South, the big, open habitat is strikingly different from the woods and thickets you're used to. To sit in the dry, stiff wind on a bald hill a mile above a river bottom and watch 30 to 50 whitetails walk out to graze wheat or alfalfa at brassy dusk, many of them sporting 120- to 150-inch racks, is almost surreal. As if to spice things up even more, you might spot a trio of mule deer, a small band of antelope or a 6x6 bull elk off in the distance.

All that is nice, but from a tangible standpoint, a Western hunt is a great way to kill your first buck of the fall. In prime states like Wyoming and Montana, the archery season opens in September. You can drive or fly out there, hunt for a week in some mighty fine weather and see a bunch of bucks. If you screw up and spook a nice 10-pointer or blow an easy shot, you'll generally get at least one or two more chances at a P&Y animal (but not always, as this is, after all, bowhunting). In the end, you have an excellent chance of shooting a big deer before your season opens back home. I can tell you this much from experience: Some big, early success in the West sure takes the pressure off the rest of your bow season. You know you're going to get some venison and at least one nice rack for the wall.

Luke Strommen lives on the Montana ranch where he guides and hunts for big bucks. "When you can watch deer 365 days a year, you learn some cool stuff," he says.

Best Early Strategies

The father-son team of Eliot and Lucas Strommen—extreme whitetailers who hunt with longbows and recurves and wooden arrows—operate a cattle ranch and an archery-only guiding service in the heart of Vandalia, Montana (population 10 or so in a good year), hard on the banks of the famous Milk River. From my experiences out there, the Strommen ranch offers some of the finest bowhunting for whitetails in the West, and anywhere in North America for that matter. The more I scout and hunt with the young and energetic Luke, the more I realize papa taught him well. The kid has whitetail knowledge beyond his years. Here's a big reason why.

"Our ranch sits smack in the middle of our hunting area, so I'm able to keep constant visual contact with our deer," says Luke. "On a daily basis, whether I'm working, guiding or hunting, I track their core bedding areas, feeding areas and travel patterns. When you watch deer 365 days a year, you're gonna learn some cool stuff."

On sultry summer mornings and evenings, Strommen drives a mile or two out over the plains, parks on a high, open ridge and scans his sprawling hunting habitat below. "It's like checking a three-dimensional aerial map in full color. I never get tired of it."

Snuggling into a rocky hillside, the guide pulls out his binoculars and spotting scope and checks the huge fields of alfalfa, corn, wheat and hay. One thing you'll find curious is that Western whitetails, even some of the mega bucks, are comfortable feeding out into large,

Out West, deer bed in the timber along rivers and walk only a couple hundred yards to feed fields. During the rut, they roam the banks for miles in search of does.

bered 100 acres, or a just a few very thick acres. All of them hold whitetails."

In any river bottom, glass for sloughs that were created by past floods or as the river changed its course over time. These riparian habitats, which are slammed full of tall cattails and willows, border the wooded points and lush hayfields and grain fields. They're almost always chocked full of whitetails and some mighty good bucks.

Take special note of this. Strommen points out that when glassing a herd in summer, you might spot an old, thick-bodied buck in an alfalfa field one afternoon. The next day, you might be surprised to see him trimming the tops off newly sprouted wheat a half-mile away on the opposite side of a river or drainage.

"This is extremely common with Western whitetails," he says. He believes that rather than having just one large core area, an old river-bottom or plains buck occupies two or even three different "sub-core areas" that are located near or adjacent to one another at various times of the fall. A resident buck spends time in each of these haunts depending on the availability of forage, his feeding desires and his physical needs from one day to the next. "I don't know that I have ever observed an old Western buck that hadn't shown some transitions between food sources throughout the course of a season," Luke adds.

Using that knowledge to full advantage, the young traditional archer has found that breaking a Western buck's large core area into smaller, more manageable sub-units increases his odds of success. "Usually, a big deer spends several days or even weeks in each area, using the same travel routes to and from his bed to his food bank. Find the areas and then the deer highways by yet more glassing and checking an aerial map. Out here, a buck might walk a thin tree line, the fringe of a clearing, the edge of a steep riverbank, any spot like that."

Hang your tree stand near a little funnel and wait. "It might take a few hours or several days for it to pay off," adds Strommen. Or you might "lose" a buck that has moved over to another food source in another sub-core area. In that case, go back to glassing, relocate the shooter and move in with another stand. Staying mobile is the key.

The Montanan's scouting routine is low impact and keeps him well out of a buck's core area prior to bow season, virtually eliminating any disturbance to a big deer's bed-to-feed pattern. "The last thing you want to

open fields well before sundown. They return to their bedding areas after sunrise each morning. "Our deer have a set path of travel for both the predominant and less-prevailing winds, as I suspect they do in other regions," notes Strommen.

You see and determine that by glassing deer as they come and go out the sides and corners of fields each day. Big Sky bucks are pretty easy to pattern—if you do your homework. Of course, things like changing food sources and hunting pressure can and will throw you some curves each fall.

Strommen glasses miles up and down the snaky Milk River, checking the brushy, timbered banks where the healthy bands of whitetails hang out. It's like that in most plains areas of the West. Whitetails are river-bottom dwellers.

Glass a river like the Milk and you'll notice how it twists and turns back and forth upon itself, creating a labyrinth of cottonwood and ash strips and pockets that tuck neatly into its folds. "We call these wooded areas 'points'," notes Strommen. "They can be a sparsely tim-

The hunting is so good in many river bottoms that you'll get multiple opportunities on a weeklong trip. I killed this 10-pointer the day after I missed a 160-inch giant.

do is put a wrinkle in a buck's security blanket and risk changing his pattern. Then you'd have to start your scouting and glassing all over again."

While Strommen has the luxury of scouting his ranch year-round, he points out that the Westerner who starts glassing for fuzzy-racked bucks on any land in late July or mid-August should be in good shape. If you're coming from back East and plan to be in country for a week or so, you should still definitely get into the glassing game. "A reasonable scenario would be to scout for two or three days before your hunt," Luke says. "In that time, you should be able to analyze the terrain, find a couple of shooters and narrow down their patterns to some degree."

Western Stands

One huge advantage of scouting in the open country is that it allows you to plan and execute your tree stand placement well in advance of bow season.

"Whitetails in my neck of the woods, bachelor groups of bucks included, seldom vary from their late-summer patterns within their sub-core areas well into September," notes Strommen. So glass a shooter in late July or August and set up early to whack him on opening day.

The guide sets a bunch of stands at least four weeks before he or his clients plan to hunt them. He is of the notion that the longer you put between the ruckus of hanging a tree stand or building a blind and the day of your bow hunt the better off you'll be. "Give a spot plenty of time for your scent to dissipate, and for disturbed deer to go back to their daily routine and get used to the stand or blind that just popped up in their area."

Out West, many good tree stand sites can be used year after year, providing there are no drastic changes in the whitetail's food sources. Some stands are most effective in September and early October; others pay off best later in the pre-rut. Some posts are good throughout bow season. In October of 2003, Strommen arrowed a great buck, "Old Massy," that he had been watching all summer. He shot him at 20 yards with his Robertson

From a ridge or bluff, glass and pattern bucks coming and going in the timber and alfalfa fields below, then move in with a tree stand for the kill. It's classic and effective archery hunting.

Stykbow from a huge wooden stand father Eliot had set up *24 years ago!*

"Quite a few guys out here have similar stories," says Luke. "Whitetail deer are, by nature, extremely habitual and *lazy* creatures. Year after year, they use the same funnels and bottlenecks. They cross the same low spot in a fence or the river. Out here, a shooter might walk 100 yards out of his way to go through an open gate. Take all that in consideration when hanging your stands, and don't think twice about setting some stands or blinds in the best locations year after year."

The Big Sky Rut

The last weeks of October and into early November are a madhouse of buck activity on the Milk River and in other regions of the wild, wild West. It offers one last chance to whack a shooter before the rut explodes and the bucks' once reliable patterns go to smithereens.

"If you spot a big 5x5 in mid to late October, be aggressive and act quickly because the old boy's hormones will soon dictate his whereabouts," says Strommen. "Bucks during this time still have a similar daily pattern, but their movements are not as predictable as they were earlier in the season."

Halloween week a few years ago found Luke switching from tree stand to blind to other stands in an effort to tag out on a sweet Pope and Young buck. The deer came to an alfalfa field like clockwork every evening—5:20, 5:23, 5:30. But every day, he took a slightly different route, staying just out of bow range. "I finally decided to set up in a tall cottonwood that seemed to be in the hub of his travels. I set the stand over my lunch hour, climbed into it at 2:00 p.m. and killed the buck at 5:22." He goes on to point out that while several other noticeably pumped-up bucks wandered back and forth to check and hassle does, the brute he shot had displayed little interest in such activities and had therefore clung to some semblance of a pattern. "The swelling in the buck's neck told me that had I waited a few more days, the deer would have gone wild,

The Milk River in Montana has long been a haven for traditional archers who shoot recurves, longbows, wooden arrows and big, fixed broadheads. Strommen hunts like that and always will.

While tree stands are most effective, once in a while you can stalk a buck along a riverbank or in a coulee that drops into a crop field.

On a recent Milk River hunt, Strommen and I paddled out with two fine bucks. Awesome!

and I'd probably never have gotten him."

Out West, scrapes can appear as early as October, but the early stuff is limited and always done by mature bucks. As in other parts of the country, scrapes pop up and go cold as food sources change and deer relocate to various feeding areas throughout October.

"Usually, the week before peak rut is the best time to hunt scrapes out here," notes Strommen. "The week of November 12 is usually prime." He goes on to say that scrape hunting can go from a good tactic to a waste of time on or about November 19, when the rut blows up on the Milk River. "Inferior bucks might hit a few scrapes, but the big boys are busy with the does." As in most other areas to the east, old Western bucks reopen some scrapes in late November and early December as they keep prowling for the last estrous gals of the year.

Strommen is not totally into scrape hunting, but when he does try it, he likes to set an ambush stand on a bottleneck, riverbank or thin strip of timber *between* two scrape lines. He likes it when big, fresh scrapes are located in two or three patches of timber separated by a narrow stretch or pocket of field. "It's not uncommon for

our bucks to cover a lot of ground, checking scrapes in several wooded areas or points. When you hunt between scrape lines, I think you double your chances of seeing many different bucks working through."

Like their kin across the country, Western bucks love to travel well downwind of their scrape lines any time of the season, taking the shortest path of least resistance as they circle and scent-check for does. That's why Strommen doesn't set up too close to fresh scrapes at first. "I think it's better to back off and hunt and observe bucks working through an area," he says. "Then move in close to the hottest scrapes and go for the kill."

For Big Sky bucks gone wild, the guide has tried scent lures with marginal success. He finds that rattling works best in the pre-rut weeks of early November. He has found that blowing a grunt tube can occasionally turn a distant buck his way, but it seldom brings one into bow range. "Grunt sparingly, even in the rut," Luke says. "More calling isn't necessarily better out here." He has actually had more luck with doe bleats. Several of Strommen's clients have bleated in bucks and run arrows through them. "I do have some confidence in deer

Look for sheds where whitetails congregate in the winter. On his ranch, Eliot Strommen picks up lots of bones in stack yards and feedlots. Lucas Strommen photo.

decoys, which rutting bucks can see a long way in the big fields and open bottoms. I've pulled in only young bucks so far, but I think it's just a matter of time until I fool a big one."

When you plan to hunt the Western rut, Strommen has some pretty standard advice. "Pack a lunch, climb into a stand early in the morning and hunt hard for as long as you can. You never know when and where a big, wild buck will show up, so go for it."

He does offer one twist though. A lot of guys he meets from back East or down South think the only place to hunt during the rut is way back in the timber near a bedding area. "But out here we have more luck hunting on the edges of fields and in nearby funnels," Luke says. "Don't be afraid to hang a stand smack on a food source where you've been spotting a lot of deer."

While the young Montanan enjoys watching big-racked brutes chase does all over the place, he tries hard to fill his one whitetail tag early in the season when bucks are much more predictable and patternable. "That's when it's easiest to set a stand and get a 20-yard shot at a big boy you've been watching for months. Plus, out here it can be a lot warmer for bowhunting in September or October than it is in November."

Shed-Hunting Secrets

You might think that after scouting all summer and hunting and guiding all fall, the guy would be ready for a break. Well, you'd be wrong. Strommen is a shed-hunting fanatic. You ought to see the bone collection, hundreds strong, in his storage closet. "For me, finding sheds is a rush," he says. "Plus, they tell me how many

Inventory your sheds and mark when and where you found them. You'll be amazed how buck patterns begin to jump out at you. Lucas Strommen photo.

and which mature bucks survived the previous hunting season."

Strommen starts looking for sheds before Christmas some years. "The earliest I've ever found one here on the Milk is December 10th and that was after an early rut. Some years the antlers start falling off closer to January."

He looks early, but not too early. "It's a sick feeling to go into an area and jump a one-horned monster," Luke says. "Who knows if he'll come back before the other big side falls off?" His goal is to find matching pairs of sheds. To do it, he advises to keep glassing until you notice few if any deer running around with headgear. Then go in and look for those precious sets.

Grid out an area, walk slowly and glass some more. Everybody uses binoculars when hunting hard-horned bucks, but hardly anybody carries them when hunting old bones. "I once sat on a log and glassed seven sheds lying around in different spots," says Strommen. "Check open fields, fence lines and open riverbanks. My favorite spot to glass is a wooded area that was just grazed by a herd of cattle. You'd be amazed how many sheds you missed on previous days or even in previous years. The cows uncover and kick up some old ones."

Always check areas where whitetails congregate in winter, like sunny, southern slopes, riverbanks or fencerows. On his ranch, Strommen finds a ton of sheds in stack yards and feedlots where deer come regularly to eat.

The Montanan sometimes saddles up and rides the woods and riverbanks. "I can't tell you how many sheds I've found from atop a horse that I walked right by days before. Antlers can be a whole lot easier to see when you look straight down for them."

Western Tips:

I fly out West from my home in Virginia because it minimizes my travel time and increases my scouting and hunting time. If you fly, you've got to be an efficient packer and choosy about the gear you take. Pack all your gear in one duffel bag (50 pounds or less to avoid an airline's excess baggage fees). Carry your bow, arrows and broadheads in a locked, hard-sided case. Sometimes it pays to ship tree stands, ladders and maybe even your duffel and bow case to your hunting destination ahead of time. UPS or FEDEX will do it for a reasonable fee. It's not a bad idea in this day and age when flying with oversize hunting gear can be costly and a big hassle.

Regardless of the weather or moon conditions, I've found that Western bucks always move earlier in the afternoons and later in the mornings than mature whitetails back in the East and South. It's one thing that makes them so fun to bowhunt! But in a place like Montana, Wyoming or eastern Colorado, a little cool weather in normally warm-to-hot September never hurts. Big deer move even earlier and more.

Whether you go for a whitetail, elk, mule deer or other big-game animal, bowhunting out West is an awesome experience.

One thing that can suppress deer activity in and around grain fields is high warm or cold winds, which are very common in the West. As compared to a calm afternoon, noticeably fewer does and bucks will parade into the alfalfa or wheat when it's blowing a gale. Some animals that do come will bed down in the grain on the lee side of a riverbank or irrigation ditch. Other deer will be spooky, running in to grab a bite and trotting back to a wind-sheltered ditch or slough. The stand hunting is always highly unpredictable on a windy day.

Before heading out on a Western adventure, check *www.weather.com* constantly to get the 10-day forecast for your hunting area. Pack accordingly and according to a checklist. You sure don't want to travel hundreds or thousands of miles only to dig in your duffel and find out you forgot your release aid, hex wrench, laser range finder, etc.

➤ Mosquitoes, gnats and other bugs can be terrible on a warm, river-bottom hunt in September or early October. Don't leave home without a good spray. No Stinking Bugs from Scent Shield works great. Available either unscented or with an earthen cover, it repels bugs but not bucks.

➤ "By early fall, groups of Western bucks have developed pecking orders," notes Strommen. "Most subordinate bucks keep walking casually on doe trails like they have all summer, while smaller groups of older bucks may or may not use those trails. Sometimes big-racked deer use their own entry and exit trails in fields. Whatever the case, other than the lone singleton, they usually still travel together." Keep all that in mind when hanging tree stands.

➤ You've got to play the horizontal winds like you would anywhere, but in many Western areas, you've got to deal with thermals that come off mountains and bench hills in the evenings as well. When cool air drops off hills and slides down into river bottoms in late afternoon, thermals become a major issue. Since there will often be several variable horizontal and vertical currents in an area, keep in mind that some spots will work well for stands, while you simply cannot hunt other places. Remember that, especially when hanging stands in the middle of the day when you can't feel the thermals. If you set up in a bad spot, thermals will come shooting down at dusk and shoot your scent straight to the bucks you're hunting.

➤ Scouting and glassing in late winter and spring is especially important out West, where some years the brutal cold, snowy and icy conditions cause a significant winter kill in certain areas. You need to find out how many deer and mature bucks survived so you can begin planning your archery strategies for the next fall. If you'll travel from back East to hunt with a rancher or outfitter, be sure to ask about the severity of the recent winters and how the whitetails have fared.

➤ Crop cycles in late summer and early fall cause whitetails to move around a bit. For example, when a farmer bales his alfalfa or harvests his barley, some does and bucks will hop over to the next lush, uncut field. Keep glassing to keep tabs on the deer and their shifting patterns.

➤ Out in the rural West, many does and some giant bucks feed, travel and even bed close to gravel country roads and dirt ranch roads. The animals are used to seeing trucks and tractors on the roads year-round, so your truck or SUV won't bother them. "Drive around and check out the natural and man-made boundaries of your hunting area, as well as the lay of the fields and timber points," advises Strommen. "Go early or late in the day and you'll get in some-low impact glassing for does and bucks."

➤ On hot, early-fall afternoons, look for bucks walking a shadowy riverbank and spilling out into the gray, shady side of a crop field.

➤ In any western state, a drastic weather change is not uncommon during archery season. One day it might be 70 and sunny; then a front will blow through with rain or snow, dropping the temperature 20, 30 or even 50 degrees. "It's important to know the tendencies of the bucks in your area according to the sudden changes," notes Strommen. "You learn that by scouting and glassing in all sorts of weather conditions."

➤ When hunting a plains habitat, glass ditches, coulees and brushy draws that rim crop fields and twist back into the vast grasslands and sage flats. Those are the travel corridors for bucks, and the places to set up a ground blind for an ambush.

➤ To make a buck hear you in big, open and windy country, blow a loud grunt tube or bleat call and bang a big set of rattling horns.

131

Chapter 14

Build A Bowhunting Paradise

I HEAR IT ALL THE TIME FROM PEOPLE across the country, "You know, I'd love to get into whitetail management, but I just hunt a few hundred acres. Heck, that's not enough ground to grow big bucks."

Well, that kind of negative thinking is your first mistake. The truth is, if you and maybe a few buddies are willing to shell out some cash and expend a considerable amount of sweat over the next few years, you can improve the health of your deer herd and maximize your archery-hunting opportunities on virtually any size tract anywhere in the country. The best part about it is that once you get your management plan off the ground, it won't take all that long before good things will happen.

In October, Terry Drury hunts green plots. Come winter, he shoots bucks in and around soybeans and corn he planted last spring.

In the following pages, four pros that have turned their few hundred acres into some of the top bowhunting grounds in America will teach you how to do it. These guys are not scientists, but hard-core archers just like you. "It's a pretty simple concept," says Neil Dougherty, the wildlife-habitat expert from western New York. "If you create better year-round food and cover for deer than the surrounding landowners have, and if you hunt your property smarter than your neighbors do each fall, you'll have the most whitetails, the most good bucks and the best hunting for miles around."

Feed First

Your first mission must be, "Plant it and they will come." But you can't just put in a few clover plots each spring and expect whitetails with mega racks to materialize out of thin air. Far too many people make that mistake. No, you need a well-devised and diverse planting plan.

For the last few years on their Iowa and Illinois farms, big-buck addicts Mark and Terry Drury have analyzed not only what the local deer eat, but more importantly what they graze and browse at various times of the year. The field data they've collected has played a key role in their food-plot strategy.

"We've found out that if we plan to bowhunt a farm a lot during the rut, we need to plant a lot of green food that deer love in October and November," says Mark. "But if we're not going to hunt a property much until December or even January, we sow a different type of feed. It costs some money and time, but you need to experiment and find out which greens and grains your deer like from September till the end of bow season."

The Drury brothers are constantly field-testing, mixing and matching greens and grains to the times when deer eat them most heavily. They don't think of it as work. It's fun and they enjoy it, and that's the attitude you need.

The current plan for the Drury's Midwestern farms is to plant green food sources like Biologic Maximum and Clover Plus heavily on lands that they'll archery hunt in October and into the breeding season. Interspersed in and around those plots, they put in some winter wheat and Buck Forage oats.

"We strip plant a lot," notes Mark. "We might sow a strip of wheat 14 feet wide, butt it up against the edge of a Maximum plot and plant another strip of oats nearby. Deer are browsers and we try to give them variety."

One thing the brothers have learned in recent years is that green is the ticket for early in the season, at least out in the Midwest. They point out that deer might walk right through a standing bean field in October to get to

Experiment and find out which greens and grains your deer prefer. Then sow a diverse lot for great hunting.

some sparkling green Biologic, whereas in cold, snowy December, they'll often run past what is left of the green to get to soybeans or corn.

While the Drurys tailor most of their early archery hunting around green fields, they never neglect the acorn crop on all their farms. Neither should you. Acorns are the primary food choice of whitetails anywhere in America. If you're not seeing many deer in your plots in October, or if all of a sudden the numbers of animals you're spotting dwindles significantly, it is highly likely that an oak tree is dropping a heavy crop of nuts close by. "Look for that tree," notes Terry. "Anytime you can bowhunt a hot oak within, say, 100 yards of a green plot, you'll see a bunch of deer."

For early-season bowhunting in the Northeast, Dougherty recommends you plant plots with a lush fall attractant like Biologic Green Patch Plus. Actually, the stuff is a great choice for September/October hunting across the country. "Just make sure to plant your plots about 45 days before the fall's first frost, depending on where you live," he says. "And make sure you've got enough moisture. The blend of wheat, oats and clover will sprout up and be thick and lush in about two weeks. Deer will find it and love it, and you can pattern and hunt bucks coming to it."

Most hunters don't own a large tractor and implements. No sweat, hire a local farmhand to disc and plant your plots one weekend.

season plots. He acknowledges that whitetails love corn, especially in the winter, "but it's a one-month wonder in most regions, and I feel like it ties up valuable soils without contributing anything to a deer's nutritional needs." The New Yorker prefers plots with green cultivars that provide whitetails with protein and other nutrients year-round.

As mentioned in Chapter 10, tall, leafy New Zealand brassica plants with 34 to 38 percent crude protein are Dougherty's secret weapon for attracting and holding deer on his Northern property in the winter months. "I sow my Biologic Maximum plots in August. Deer might not use those plots until the starch in the brassicas turns to sugar when it gets cold in December. But then you'll have an amazing late-season spot, especially considering how the brassicas seem to draw more bucks than does."

Archery Plots

Each spring, the Drurys sow plots and strips designed for one thing: To provide awesome encounters with Midwestern monsters 7 or 8 months down the road. For post-rut hunting, they plant mostly corn and soybeans. Rut-weary and famished deer flock to those high-carb foods, especially the beans, in December, particularly when it's brutally cold and snowy. They also sow some green feed, like Biologic Cover Plus or Maximum, in and around the crops.

"When ponds and creeks freeze in December out here, there's very little green forage around," points out Mark. "Biologic becomes attractive and provides deer with a good source of moisture." Drury goes on to say that he believes the water content of greens is a big attractant for whitetails during winter dry spells.

The Drurys believe that if you plant a good variety of corn, soybeans and Biologic, you'll see many if not most of the deer that live on your land, and you'll also pull bucks from surrounding properties. Deep into the season when all the acorns and other natural forage are pretty much history, and when the guns start booming on your neighbors' lands, your ground will become a haven for whitetails. Does and bucks will come from all directions to escape the pressure and especially for the food.

Dougherty takes a different approach for his late-

Say "food plot" and your average hunter envisions a shimmering green patch of 3 to 5 acres or more, or maybe a huge field of corn, soybeans or alfalfa that is sure to attract a lot of deer at various times during bow season. Well, large plots and fields might be okay for gun hunters, but when you're trying to kill a mega buck with stick and string at 30 yards or less, you need to narrow things down, *way down*.

Dougherty's specialty is to design, build and plant green plots of *an acre or less* for close encounters with bucks. He positions his tiny, irregularly shaped plots across a property to take full advantage of the predominant winds and the best cover. "The closer you plant to thick stuff, the better chance an old buck will show up to eat while there's still enough light left to shoot," he notes.

The pro has designed several signature plots. The "See-Through Hourglass" is one of his favorites. It is a great example of how to get creative when planting exclusively for bowhunting.

The plot is just under an acre, with two round "glasses" necked down to 30 yards in the middle. The plan is for deer to walk into the neck, see through to both ends of the plot, feel safe and then go about feeding on the greens. To help make that happen, Dougherty piles trees and brush that he dozed and cut when build-

ing a plot on the upwind side of the neck. The barriers and edge help to direct and funnel some animals down into the center of the plot.

"Also, many old does and bucks will try to enter a plot with their noses in the wind," he notes. "So I build another windrow 60 to 70 yards long and directly behind my main bow stand. It helps to block the deer and force them in on an upwind side." Dougherty also hangs an alternate stand on the opposite side of the neck and hunts that one when the wind changes.

I should point out that while Dougherty's bowhunting plots are small, he recommends that you plant at least one major "feeding plot" of around 5 acres in a mostly woodland habitat. Seed it with 60 percent perennial and 40 percent annual plants for max productivity year-round. He really likes a Biologic blend of clover, chicory and brassica. In a good, moist year, a plot this size should grow some 40 tons of high-protein forage, much of it up and available during the critical spring and summer months when bucks grow antlers and does lactate.

"Try to leave your major plot alone," advises Dougherty. "Rarely if ever hunt it. Let all that feed pull deer from all around." He point outs that does and bucks will feel safe and like hanging out on your land.

While the Drurys plant some large to huge crop fields on their properties each spring, they also narrow things down by configuring inner terrains for bowhunting. For example, they might plant corn or soybeans 30 yards off a wood line where they have a bow stand, or near a particular tree where they plan on hanging one next fall. In the 30 yards of open ground between the grain and the stand, they plant a strip of green, maybe a combination of clover and Biologic Maximum, or Buck Forage oats and Maximum. They pour the fertilizer to the green plants closest to their stand.

"A lot of evenings deer come out and browse down the fringe of grain and into the low, green plants," notes Mark. "The edge of the grain, especially if it's standing corn, and the timber line create a funnel right to your stand."

Another interesting thing the brothers do is to frost seed clover or Biologic Clover Plus in February or March. If over the course of a season they spotted quite a few deer moving in, around or through an overgrown pasture that is too steep, rocky or inaccessible to plow, they walk in and sprinkle seeds within 50 yards or so of where they have a bow stand or plan to hang one next season. They always try to frost seed near the thickest bedding cover in an area because that is where old, big deer are most likely to move in daylight hours. "Some of the clover will take, and you'll have a great, out-of-the-way food source for deer next fall," notes Terry.

Jim Crumley is another die-hard bowhunter with a passion for managing whitetails. When the Trebark cre-

For more shots at bucks, pour the fertilizer to clover and other greens within 40 yards of your tree stands.

When clearing plots, build windrows nearby that will funnel deer close to and upwind of your tree stands.

ator bought his 296-acre property hard on the banks of the James River near Roanoke, Virginia, in 1991, it was all ridges and woods, with one 20-acre overgrown field seemingly tossed into the middle for good measure. Crumley did what most of us would have done back then. He mowed the field—"scalped it really," he says—

135

A 4x4 ATV is your workhorse. Use it to disc, plant, fertilize ... and haul out the does and bucks you shoot later in the year.

and planted it all in ladino clover. The plants grew beautifully, shimmering green like a golf course in late spring. People would come by and see that field and say, "Well, that's just beautiful," he recalls.

One day, a biologist with the Virginia DMAP program came out to survey his land. He was not so impressed. "You know, Jim, you'd do you and the deer a lot better to strip plant that field." Crumley had never thought of that, but he was game to try it.

These days in that field, the Virginian discs and plants a strip of clover or a Biologic blend about two tractor cuts wide and 300 yards long. He then leaves a four-tractor-wide strip of natural vegetation—blackberry, honeysuckle and the like—before moving over and planting another green strip. He goes on like that until all 20 acres are lined with green strips and tangles of native browse.

It has worked out wonderfully. "For one thing, other than an annual fall planting and some fertilizing, the strips are low maintenance and cost-effective," Crumley says. "Today, a lot of busy hunters will appreciate that.

Oh yeah, the deer love those strips too."

What the biologist told Crumley was on the money. "Of course deer will graze clover, Biologic or whatever green groceries you plant for them, but they absolutely love to browse, too," he notes. "The best and easiest way to give the animals that browse is to simply leave edges and strips of native vegetation and fertilize them once a year. For example, it's amazing how in October deer eat the leaves of the blackberries I treat. They just love them."

For archery hunting throughout bow season, the Virginia pro hangs nine or 10 stands along the perimeter of the strip-planted field. This gives him plenty of options according to how the winds and deer patterns change. Whether tight to a green strip or native vegetation, almost all of those stands are automatic, at least for shots at does.

Here's one more easy and financially feasible way to line your woods with prime deer feed. Roll in with your ATV and mow, plow, seed and fertilize any and all logging roads that might cut your property. "Planting 1000 yards of road is equal to putting in a one-acre food plot," notes Dougherty. Many logging roads are flat and open and have easy access, so sowing them with a high-quality perennial is a no-brainer. Dougherty recommends Biologic Clover Plus, a clover/chicory blend with about 25 percent protein. The long, winding green strips should grow well for 4 or 5 years, even in dry times, and especially help to nourish lactating does and antler-growing bucks from spring through August. Greens tend to grow best on north-south roads that receive 3 to 4 hours of sunlight each day, "but plant as many roads as you can for maximum food tonnage and edge for your deer," says Neil.

Sanctuaries

Dougherty advises to put at least 20 percent of your land off limits to human intrusion. A "sanctuary" or major bedding/security area may be 5 to 20 acres. "Size doesn't matter, but the type of cover sure does," he notes.

A sanctuary should be so thick and gnarly that a buck can lie in a bed and never see you walk or ride by on a quad at 30 yards. It might be a 6-year-old clear-cut, cedar thicket, a pine plantation in the South—you get

the idea. You might also designate a steep, rough, wind-swirling spot as a sacred ground for deer. You can't hunt it effectively, so why not turn it over to the bucks?

It is a good idea to establish at least one large, primary sanctuary in or near the center of your property. No matter the wind direction each day, bucks can move easily out from the bedding cover to the food plots or strips you have scattered around. Also, when the guns start booming on surrounding lands in November or December, many does and bucks scared out of their wits will jump the fence, pile into your sanctuary and hold there, deep on your land, for the rest of bow season.

In addition, designate a few satellite sanctuaries in various corners of your woods. They'll provide bucks with convenient "rest stops" as they move out to feed or nose for does.

After earmarking a sanctuary, your goal is to never step foot in it—no hiking, no working, no scouting, no anything— most days of the year. "One day in August I might go into a thicket and drop 10 to 15 trees to grow the sanctuary a little more and to create more browse for deer that season," notes Dougherty. He might go in one day in January and scout for old buck sign and sheds. But that's it. "You certainly never want to hunt in or too close to one of your

A utilization cage lets you see how deer are feeding in your plots. If they're munching greens outside the cage down to the ground, you probably need to put in more plots and shoot more does. If the animals aren't eating much, plant another type of seed.

A great and easy way to feed deer is to disc and plant old logging roads. Sowing 1000 yards of road with clover is like putting in a 1-acre food plot.

Build A Bowhunting Paradise

Design, build and plant small food plots and strips for archery hunting. Keep an area's predominant winds in mind as you configure a plot's edges and necked-down funnels.

To see more old bucks in shooting light, sow your plots near thick cover.

sanctuaries. To do that would blow your plan of holding deer on your small piece of land."

The Drurys are also big believers in sanctuaries, and they establish multiple no-hunting zones on all their properties, be it 70 acres or a 500-acre tract. "Along with the cover, you've got to have feed," notes Mark. "If there isn't a good, abundant food source nearby, you can't hold a good number of animals in a cover, no matter how thick and secluded it might be. If the eats are not there, the deer are not going to stay there."

With sanctuaries established near food sources, you need to hang stands and hunt them smartly. For afternoon hunts, the Drurys like to set up on the edges of food plots and along travel corridors back toward a security cover. "We'll bowhunt a stand like that only on the perfect wind," notes Terry. "But it sure is a good way to hunt a mature buck we know is working an area without exerting too much pressure on him."

Sometimes, depending on the situation and the lay of the land, the brothers hunt the edge of a sanctuary either morning or afternoon. They key on any natural edges that deer might use when going or coming from bed to feed. "Bucks love to walk the edge of timber, checking for does going in and out of a bedding area," says Mark. "That's a good spot to be 20 feet up a tree, but only when the wind is right. And keep this in mind. If you see a big deer moving to or from a bedding

In spring, spray and fertilize apple and other soft-mast trees. In fall, hunt for a buck fattening up on all the sweet fruits you grow.

area—especially if he's going toward it in the morning—nine times out of 10 he'll circle downwind of that cover and check it before he steps inside."

Diversity is Key

I bet you've never read this before: A chainsaw is one of the bowhunter's best tools. Dougherty is forever firing his up, felling trash trees from 20 inches on down, opening up some of the canopy in the woods and creating swaths that will receive plenty of sunlight. "Soon after a cutting, forbs and brambles pop up. For the next few years, deer feed will flourish in the cuts—forbs,

Build A Bowhunting Paradise

briers, berry bushes, tree shoots and the like. Also, the treetops you leave will provide deer with browse the first year and good cover for years to come."

The New Yorker creates yet more deer feed and cover with "living brush piles," many of which line the planted logging roads on his land. To make them, saw strips of 3- to 6-inch trees and shrubs, but don't cut all the way to sever them from the stumps. Just saw through the trunks until the tops topple over. They'll live for one or 2 years or longer and provide abundant and reachable browse for deer. Alive and then dead, the felled trees will offer great cover for does and bucks—and also for you as you slip down an old road to scout or hang a bow stand.

While you're out there with your saw, scout for old apple, persimmon, paw-paw or other soft-mast trees hidden in the woods. Then "open" them up. Clear brush and trash trees that choke a fruit tree, and it will soon get more sunlight, flourish and make more sweets. Hang a tree stand nearby for yet another early-season honey hole.

Finally, you might want to plant some mast trees, especially if long-term habitat management is on your agenda. In 1992, Crumley purchased and planted 50 saw-tooth oak seedlings on his Virginia property. He clustered 30 trees in one area, and scattered the rest around. They've done great. "Some trees produced acorns in the eighth fall," he says. "By the 12th year, the trees were eight to 10 feet tall, and all but four of them were bearing."

Post and patrol your property to keep poachers out and to keep others from disturbing the deer.

The best part about saw-tooth oaks is that unlike other native white and red oaks, they bear a reliable crop of nuts each year. "They fall in mid to late September, and deer feed on them through October, so you've got some great bowhunting opportunities," notes Crumley. "If I had it to do over again, I'd plant a lot more saw-tooths, especially in open areas where they'd get a lot of sun."

Planting some oak or apple trees and maybe some pines for added cover on your land requires an investment of time and money, but it can be the final link in your overall diversity plan. "If your deer have plenty of cover and plenty of plants and mast to eat year-round, and if they're not pressed too much by dogs, predators or hunters, the animals will feel safe and hang around on your property, even if it's pretty darn small," says Crumley. "Of course, the longer they're there, the better your chances of killing a good buck with your bow."

Hunt Smart

Over the course of several weekends, hop on your ATV, strap on your chainsaw and ride all your property lines to establish a quad trail that encircles the perimeter of your tract. Ride or walk those trails year-round—when tacking up posted signs, planting in the spring, scouting in late summer and on and on. During bow season, the trails will provide quick, easy and quiet access to your tree stands or ground blinds.

"The more time you spend on the trails the better," notes Dougherty. "Your presence tells people on the neighboring lands that you are out there a lot, hunting, watching and keeping tabs on your property."

Here are a few other ways to maximize your investment of time, money and sweat:

1. Rather than wandering all over the woods and unwittingly kicking deer off your property, stick to main logging roads and your ATV trails as much possible, especially during hunting season.

2. Try to hang your bow stands within 150 yards or so of logging roads or trails to prevent clumping too far through the woods and spooking deer.

3. Always sneak silently into stands from somewhere downwind. Use fallen trees, windrows, conifer rows, plot edges and the like for silent access and cover. Try to never walk through bedded or feeding deer.

4. As mentioned, never scout or hunt in a sanctuary. Skirt covers so that your scent never blows into them.

5. Shoot your legal limit of does but not in or around the plots where you plan to hunt a mega buck. Designate a couple of doe-shooting areas away from your best big-deer core areas.

You'll probably never be able to kill enough does with bows to get the sex ratio of your whitetail herd in check. You and your friends should pick up your guns and shoot some does near the end of the season. But again, try not to shoot in or near a plot or cover where bucks are recuperating in the post-rut.

6. Pass on 1½- and 2½-year-old bucks and try to convince hunters on neighboring lands to do likewise.

7. Limit the number of hunters and the days of pressure on your land. When the guns start booming on adjacent properties, watch for does and bucks leaping the fences and pouring into your sanctuaries. Stay smart and you can bow hunt those bucks on your land for the rest of the season.

Deer Habitat Tips:

➤ Before you plant the first seed, get a soil test. Log onto *www.mossyoakbiologic.com* and click on "Soil Test." Download and fill out one form and send it, along with a soil sample and a small fee, to the Biologic Lab. Within 36 hours, the lab will analyze your soil and get back with you via fax or email with liming and planting recommendations.

➤ Across your property, design and plant a variety of spring and fall plots. Spring plots provide nutrition for lactating does and bucks growing antlers. Fall plots attract deer and are generally your best bowhunting plots.

➤ In the spring, plant plots when the daytime temperature consistently reaches the 70s, which means the soil temperature should be in the 60s. Plant fall plots as early as possible in late summer, but make sure there is enough rain to germinate the seeds (it's mighty dry in August in many areas). Planting fall plots from mid-August to mid-September is pretty typical. Don't wait too long; you need to plant your plots well before the first frost.

➤ You've got to put your food plots where there is adequate soil moisture to germinate the seeds. Try to plant a plot so that it runs north/south. There will be enough sun to grow plants, but also plenty of shade so the plot won't bake too much.

➤ "Small plots and strips work well, but when your fall plantings come up, deer can eat them quickly," notes Jim Crumley. "Each year, you need to monitor things and keep pace with the deer if you have to. When you manage your land, you attract more and more whitetails, so you might have to plant more and more plots and strips."

➤ Leave pockets or strips of pines or cedars in and around plots or strips. Those will act as windbreaks in the winter, and provide deer with some shade in the summer.

➤ The Biologic professionals say to disc the soil and then prepare a firm seedbed. Don't plant

Before you plant one seed, get the soil tested. A lab will give you advice on what to plant and how much lime and fertilizer you need.

the seeds too deep. Cover seeds with no more than a quarter-inch of soil.

➤ Like most hunters, you probably don't own a 50 or 100 hp tractor and large implements. Try to hire a local farmhand to brush-hog, plow and plant a large crop field or major feeding plot.

➤ Invest $500 or so in a heavy-duty chainsaw; an axe and wedges; and a safety helmet, chaps, goggles and earplugs. Then get to work. "Everybody talks about food plots, but cutting

strips and clearings is every bit as important because it creates a diversity of food and cover for deer," says Neil Dougherty. Use your saw for opening roads, clearing wind-fallen trees and 100 other jobs.

➤ A 4x4 ATV is your workhorse. Use it to seed logging roads and to put in food plots of an acre or less. Shop for an all-in-one ATV implement that features a disc, dragger, seed/fertilizer spreader and roller. You'll also need a 25-gallon sprayer attachment for treating food plots and strips with a herbicide like Roundup. A pull-behind mower is great for clipping plots, road edges and hunter-access trails. Remove the implements and use your quad for scouting, patrolling and hauling out dead deer.

➤ To read more about Neil Dougherty's innovative habitat methods check out his book, *Grow 'Em Right: A Guide to Creating Habitat and Food Plots.* Go online at *www.NorthCountry Whitetails.com* or call (315) 331-6959.

➤ You'll also find some great management advice in *Giant Whitetails* by Mark and Terry Drury and co-authored by yours truly. To order, contact KP Books (1-800-258-0929).

Brush-hog old fields and woodland openings in late summer. New forbs and other native plants will pop up for deer to browse. Many animals will walk in the mowed strips, so hang a few stands nearby.

A 25-gallon sprayer for your ATV comes in very handy when it comes time to treat plots with herbicides and pesticides.

EXPERT INSIGHT
for Whitetail Hunters

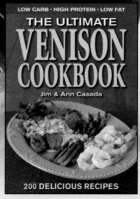

Strategic Whitetail Hunting
by Tim Hooey

Learn techniques from expert hunter Tim Hooey (host of the North American Fish & Game TV show) on how to plan for the hunt and adapt your strategy to a specific territory. This easy-to-read guide reviews important traits of the whitetail biology, explores equipment selection and scouting techniques, and discusses planning-based techniques for whitetail harvesting.

Softcover • 6 x 9 • 224 pages
100 b&w photos • 8-page color section
Item# SWH • $19.99

Modern Whitetail Hunting
by Michael Hanback

With advice from one of the foremost hunting writers in the world today, learn where mature bucks live and what triggers their movements, best early and late-season strategies, up-to-date tree stand, rattling, calling, and scent tricks, how to hunt huge deer on small lands, and much more. Get the advice of Mossy Oak's top big-buck hunters. More than 100 photographs and illustrations set into motion today's latest and greatest whitetail strategies.

Softcover • 6 x 9 • 224 pages
100 b&w photos • 8-page color section
Item# MWH • $19.99

The Ultimate Venison Cookbook
200 Delicious Recipes
by Jim & Ann Casada

Venison fans will love this new cookbook, featuring 200 fabulous venison recipes! It discusses important tips and techniques for dressing, processing and preparing venison for cooking. The recipes cover a wide range of dishes, from soups to grilled meals and much more. Includes a discussion of the health benefits of venison and a selection of low-carb recipes.

Comb-bound • 6 x 9 • 208 pages
Item# CVCV2 • $14.99

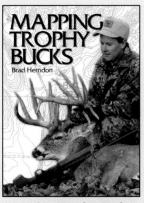

Mapping Trophy Bucks
Using Topographic Maps to Find Deer
by Brad Herndon

Remain one step ahead of the competition! The next time out in the field, the odds will be in your favor if you have a topographical map. With this new guide, you will learn the basic concepts of topographical maps and implementing sound terrain hunting strategies. From inside corners and double inside corners to the perfect funnel and mastering the wind, get a better concept of using the wind and understanding topographical maps. Illustrations show details of how deer move, where to place your stand, and how to use the wind to ensure a successful whitetail hunt.

Softcover • 8-1/4 x 10-7/8 • 192 pages
150 color photos
Item# TRTT • $24.99

Benoit Bucks
Whitetail Tactics for a New Generation
by Bryce M. Towsley

This highly anticipated follow-up volume details the "second generation" of the Benoit family, brothers Shane, Lanny, and Lane, established trophy deer hunters who are every bit as successful as their legendary father. Adventure stories recount the excitement of the chase, sharing the secret strategies that led to success-or sometimes failure-and most importantly, what was learned from those hunting experiences. Detailed accounts tie humor with solid teaching on the fundamentals of whitetail hunting.

Hardcover • 8-1/4 x 10-7/8 • 224 pages
150 b&w photos • 16-page color section
Item# HBB2 • $29.99

Giant Whitetails
A Lifetime of Lessons
by Mark and Terry Drury

Leave it up to the high-adventure outdoor team of Mark and Terry Drury to reveal hidden secrets others would not tell! From how to hunt rare October cold fronts and utilizing ultimate deer funnels, to hunting mature bucks in their own bedroom, Giant Whitetails discloses revealing facts on consistently harvesting trophy bucks. The Drury's share observation tactics and tips for hunting by the moon, as well as methods for successful ground hunting, non-intrusive hunting, and using rattling antlers effectively.

Hardcover • 8-1/4 x 10-7/8 • 240 pages
340 color photos
Item# WWDH • $29.99

kp books
Offer OTB4

An imprint of F+W Publications, Inc.
P.O. Box 5009, Iola WI 54945-5009
www.krausebooks.com

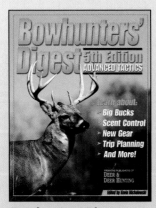
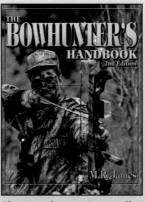
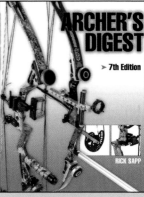